From Freeman's Ford to Bentonville

1st Lt. John Arbuckle, Company B, 61st Ohio Volunteer Infantry
Portrait in possession of Robert G. Carroon

From Freeman's Ford to Bentonville

The 61st Ohio Volunteer Infantry

Edited with an Introduction
by
Robert G. Carroon

Civil War Heritage Series – Volume XII

BURD STREET PRESS

Copyright © 1998 by Robert G. Carroon

ALL RIGHTS RESERVED—No part of this book may be reproduced in any form without permission in writing from the publisher, except by a reviewer who wishes to quote brief passages in connection with a review.

This Burd Street Press publication
was printed by
Beidel Printing House, Inc.
63 West Burd Street
Shippensburg, PA 17257-0152 USA

In respect for the scholarship contained herein, the acid-free paper used in this book meets the guidelines for permanence and durability of the Committee on Production Guidelines for Book Longevity of the Council on Library Resources.

For a complete list of available publications
please write
Burd Street Press
Division of White Mane Publishing Company, Inc.
P.O. Box 152
Shippensburg, PA 17257-0152 USA

Library of Congress Cataloging-in-Publication Data

From Freeman's Ford to Bentonville : the 61st Ohio Volunteer Infantry
    edited with an introduction by Robert G. Carroon.
        p.   cm. -- (Civil War heritage series ; v. 12)
    Includes index.
    ISBN 1-57249-077-2 (alk. paper)
    1. United States. Army. Ohio Infantry Regiment, 61st (1862-1865)
    2. Ohio--History--Civil War, 1861-1865--Regimental histories.
    3. United States--History--Civil War, 1861-1865--Regimental
    histories. I. Carroon, Robert G. (Robert Girard)   II. Series.
    E525.5 61st F76   1998
    973.7'471--dc21   98-17945
                                                                    CIP

PRINTED IN THE UNITED STATES OF AMERICA

In Memory of
First Lieutenant John Arbuckle
Company B, 61st Ohio Volunteer Infantry
and for the
Companions of the Connecticut, Ohio, and Wisconsin Commanderies
Military Order of the Loyal Legion of the United States
and Alden Skinner Camp #45
Sons of Union Veterans of the Civil War

Contents

Acknowledgements	viii
Introduction	
by Robert G. Carroon	1
The Sixty-first Ohio Volunteers, 1861–1865	
by Frederick Stephens Wallace	16
The Battle of Chancellorsville	
by James H. Peabody	41
From Stafford Heights to Gettysburg in 1863	
by Leonidas M. Jewett	47
Report on the Battle of Gettysburg	
by William H. H. Bown	54
The Boys in Blue at Missionary Ridge	
by Leonidas M. Jewett	58
Lydon of Andersonville	
by John McElroy	63
Index	67

Acknowledgements

Thanks are due to many who assisted in the preparation of this volume on the 61st Ohio Volunteer Infantry, especially Dr. Richard J. Sommers and Michael J. Winey of the United States Military History Institute, Carlisle Barracks, Pennsylvania; LTC Thomas P. Curtis; Anne B. Shepherd of the Cincinnati Historical Society; Gary J. Arnold of the Archives Division, Ohio Historical Society; Timothy K. Nenninger and Michael Musick of the Military Reference Branch, National Archives; Dr. David G. Martin of Longstreet House, and Charles "Chip" Rogers of the University of Ohio at Athens and the Ohio Department, Sons of Union Veterans of the Civil War. A special word of gratitude to Gregory Kendall Bakker, Malcolm Douglas Girardeau, John Philip Girardeau, Jerry Leachy, Michael Patrick Sullivan and Lee Allen Tryon for their friendship and for accompanying me on many a battlefield and research excursion. Errors of both commission and omission are my own.

Robert G. Carroon
West Hartford, Connecticut

Introduction

By Dr. Robert G. Carroon
Commander in Chief, Military Order of the Loyal Legion of the United States and great-grandson of John Arbuckle, formerly First Lieutenant 61st Ohio Volunteers

The 61st Ohio Volunteer Infantry was a fairly typical regiment in the Union army in the Civil War. It was unusual in that it served in the Army of the Potomac and then in the Army of the Cumberland and was present at such major engagements as Second Bull Run, Fredericksburg, Chancellorsville, and Gettysburg as well as Missionary Ridge, the Chattanooga-Atlanta Campaign, and the March to the Sea. The 61st was particularly hard hit at Freeman's Ford (its first engagement) and Second Bull Run, Chancellorsville, Gettysburg, and Peachtree Creek. It fought its final battle at Bentonville, North Carolina, on March 18, 1865.

The regiment was formed at Camp Chase, Columbus, Ohio, on April 23, 1862. It comprised recruits from all parts of Ohio (including transplanted Yankees from Connecticut), Indiana, Kentucky and newly arrived immigrants, chiefly Irish, Scots, and German. Because the regiment's commanding officer through most of the war, Colonel Stephen Joseph McGroarty, was Irish it is often thought of as an Irish regiment, but that is not the case. By the same token because it was in the XI Corps in the Army of the Potomac it is often lumped in with the German regiments, and is subjected to the same criticism that they received particularly for Chancellorsville and Gettysburg.

The 61st was originally commanded by Newton Schleich and followed the daily routine which he devised for training and indoctrination into the ways of the army. The daily routine at Camp Chase was as follows: 5:00 A.M., Reveille and Roll Call; 6:00 A.M., Breakfast; 6:30 A.M., Morning Reports; 7:00 A.M., Surgeon's Call; 7:00 A.M.–8:00 A.M., Officers' Call; 8:00 A.M. Guard Mounting; 9:00 A.M.–10:00 A.M., Squad Drill; 10:30 A.M.–12:00 P.M., Company Drill; 12:00 P.M., Dinner; 2:00 P.M.–4:00 P.M., Battalion Drill (first call for same, 1:30 P.M.); 5:30 P.M.,

Dress Parade; 6:00 P.M., Supper; 7:00 P.M., Retreat; 9:00 P.M., Tattoo; 9:30 P.M., Taps. Colonel Schleich had the routine copied in the Regimental Order Book and followed it rigorously. The regiment was also privileged to have, for a brief period, a band which had been raised in Lancaster, Ohio, but was mustered out on April 28, 1862, prior to the troops' departure for action.

During their stay at Camp Chase, by then a prisoner of war camp, the men of the 61st served as prison camp guards. This was not to Colonel Schleich's liking and he wrote on several occasions to General John C. Fremont asking that the regiment be ordered into active service in Virginia.

A month after the 61st arrived at Camp Chase it left its encampment for the field in western Virginia where it joined the army of Major General John C. Fremont on June 22, 1862, at Strasburg and marched with that army across the Blue Ridge to Sperryville, Virginia. At this point General Fremont was relieved of command and succeeded by Major General John Pope. From Sperryville the 61st, which was part of the 1st Brigade, 2nd Division of the I Corps, marched to the vicinity of Cedar Mountain, but did not reach the field in time to participate in the battle.

The Morning Report for August 2, 1862, taken at Sperryville, Virginia, showed ten companies with 3 field officers, 4 regimental officers, 21 company officers, and 586 enlisted men present for duty. Five company officers and 83 enlisted men were reported sick. Absent on assigned duty were 4 officers and 47 enlisted men. One hundred sixty-one men were AWOL. The regiment had 37 commissioned officers and 877 enlisted men for an aggregate of 914. There were also 72 serviceable horses.

The 61st crossed the Rappahannock River on August 22, 1862, and engaged a Confederate force on the southside of the river. The Confederate force consisted initially of Brigadier General Isaac R. Trimble's Brigade. Trimble was reinforced by two brigades under Brigadier Generals John Bell Hood and Evander M. Law (Whiting's Brigade). The 61st was forced back across the Rappahannock at Freeman's Ford and in the engagement the brigade commander, Brigadier General Henry Bohlen, was killed. In the action the 61st lost five killed, one mortally wounded, and six wounded. Among the wounded was Second Lieutenant John Arbuckle of Company H, the first officer to become a casualty. He was only slightly wounded, however, being hit in the right hand, and was with the regiment when it went into action at the battle of Second Bull Run seven days later. The first enlisted man, and first member of the regiment to fall in battle was apparently Alfred H. Rallston.

In his report on the action the commanding officer of Company A, Frederick S. Wallace, wrote, "The enemy opened on us with his artillery.

Col. and Bvt. Brig. Gen. Stephen J. McGroarty
Mass. MOLLUS Collection, USAMHI

On the 24th our regiment lay under the fire of three of his batteries for the period of an hour and then marched a distance of a half a mile under a most severe cross fire of several batteries without a loss in this Company." Company C was not so fortunate. Captain David W. Crouse reported that they were "engaged in a severe skirmish in which the company lost two killed and two wounded near Freeman's Ford on the Rappahannock River, Va. Aug. 24th was exposed for two hours to Heavy Cannonading at White Sulpher Springs, Va."

In addition to being its first fight Freeman's Ford was significant in the history of the regiment because almost immediately following the battle the lieutenant colonel, Stephen J. McGroarty, was appointed to command, succeeding Colonel Newton Schleich. Colonel Schleich, according to reports in the Official Records, was nowhere to be found during the battle, the implication being that he was either intoxicated, a coward, or possibly both. On September 20, Colonel Schleich wrote Colonel Alexander Schimmelfennig tending his resignation stating, "The reasons which impel me to this act are, frankly, that the relations between myself and some few of the officers of the Regt. are such, that the public service must be prejudiced by our all remaining in the same regiment." The endorsements by the officers up the chain of command showed an embarrassing rush to get Schleich out of the army: "Approved and urgently recommended" wrote Schimmelfennig. Major General Carl Schurz noted, "Approved and very urgently recommended to Major General Sigel." Franz Sigel was a little more restrained, as befitting a corps commander, but not much, writing that he was forwarding the resignation "with the recommendation that the resignation of Col. Schleich be accepted immediately, tending as it would to the interest of the service." Three days after he wrote out his resignation Major General George B. McClellan gave the former colonel of the 61st an honorable discharge and Newton Schleich was out of the army, never to reappear. Colonel McGroarty remained in command of the 61st for the duration of the war, only being absent on furlough or when recovering from the loss of his left arm at Peachtree Creek two years later.

On August 23 and 24 the 61st had another fight with elements of Lieutenant General James Longstreet's Corps at Sulphur Springs, Virginia, in which it took some casualties. On August 25 it had a brisk skirmish at Waterloo Bridge. David C. Beckett, commanding Company F, noted that their task was to burn the bridge at Waterloo and they succeeded. On the same night the 61st fell back to Warrenton, and remained there until August 27. From Warrenton it fell back with the Union army and took part in the Battle of Second Bull Run. Captain Beckett in describing the action of Company F at Second Bull Run, wrote in his report, "On Friday we engaged the enemy and were under constant fire for nine hours. On Saturday our Regiment was ordered to support Dilger's Battery which it did until ordered off the field about 9 o'clock. It was the last Regiment to leave the field." Captain Frederick S. Wallace describes the participation of the 61st in some detail. He is particularly critical of Major General Fitz John Porter's failure to support Pope in the action. Following the battle the regiment covered the retreat of the Union army on Centerville Turnpike toward Washington, D.C. In the Battle of Second Bull Run the 61st lost twenty-five men killed and wounded and had seven missing or captured. Major General Carl Schurz commented on the 61st after the battle that it was "a regiment which throughout the whole campaign had exhibited the most commendable spirit."

On September 2 the regiment was engaged in a skirmish with the enemy at Fairfax Court House or Chantilly, Virginia. On that day the Morning Report listed 8 companies with 400 enlisted men and 12 officers. Two hundred sixty-three soldiers were AWOL or missing and 150 were on other duty, giving the regiment an aggregate of 886 men. It again fell back to the Chain Bridge where it was encamped lying between Washington and Centerville until October 2, 1862. It was then assigned to the XI Corps under Major General Franz Sigel as a part of the reserve force of 47,000 troops under Major General Nathaniel P. Banks which was ordered to protect the capital. Because of this assignment the 61st did not participate in the Battle of Antietam.

On November 1 the 61st moved through Thorofare Gap to the Rappahannock and to Warrenton; then returned to Centerville. Having been in command for approximately three months Colonel McGroarty reorganized the regiment and brought it up to strength. On December 10 it started, under orders, for Fredericksburg, but arrived too late to participate in Major General Ambrose Burnside's attack on that place. From Falmouth, Virginia, the regiment fell back to Aquia Creek and went into winter quarters.

While in camp near Aquia Creek on January 5, 1863, Colonel McGroarty reported to General Schimmelfennig that "on or about the 18th day of December the Rev. J. E. P. Corcoran, Chaplain of this, the Sixty-first Regt O.V.I. with Messers Brown and Moore, Sutlers, of the Regiment was taken prisoner by the enemy at or near Dumfries, Va when on his way to Washington with leave and on official business."

The regiment marched to Hartwood Church on January 20, 1863, and constructed winter quarters, but after sleeping in them only one night was ordered to abandon them and march to Stafford Court House. At that place the men again built winter quarters and this time remained in them until April 27, 1863. We can only speculate what caused Colonel McGroarty to issue Regimental Order No. 13 on March 30, 1863: "It is hereby ordered that Frederick Blumenthal, Chief of Drum Corps be reduced to the Ranks and that J. Smith, Bugler, assume duties as Chief of Drum Corps." On April 14, 1863, the colonel issued Regimental

Order No. 21 which showed how the 61st was prepared to go into action. "Commandants of Companies will have their Commands in readiness to march tomorrow morning at 9 o'clock precisely. Three days cooked rations will be carried in the haversacks by the men and 5 days rations of Hard bread, Coffee, Sugar and Salt in their knapsacks. The canteen must be filled with water."

The 61st on April 27 crossed the Rappahannock at Kelly's Ford, and moved to the rear of the Confederate position at Fredericksburg, where it formed a connection with that portion of the Union army which had crossed the Rappahannock at United States Ford. It took position on the right preparatory to the Battle of Chancellorsville, which began at six o'clock in the evening of May 2. The 61st was engaged on May 2, 3, 4 and 5. Stephen Sears in his book, *Chancellorsville,* reports that the 61st, which had behaved quite well in supporting Captain Herbert Dilger's battery (reduced eventually to one piece) lost 33 men killed, and 27 wounded, including four officers. Chancellorsville was a battle that left a lasting scar on all the XI Corps, including the men of the 61st. As Wallace indicates the veterans spent the rest of their lives dealing with the issue of their failure and that of their commander, Major General Oliver O. Howard. Even more devastating than Wallace in his criticism of Howard is Sergeant J. H. Peabody of Company B of the 61st who describes the general's confusion and egocentric attitude on the battlefield in a paper delivered before the GAR Post in Cincinnati, Ohio in 1903.

On May 6 the regiment fell back to its old quarters at Stafford Court House remaining there until June 12. The men then joined in the pursuit of Lee's army which was at that time making its way into Pennsylvania. At Gettysburg, on July 1 it formed part of the 1st Brigade, 3rd Division, XI Army Corps, Army of the Potomac. At the commencement of the action there were only 143 (this is Warren Hassler's estimate; the 61st monument on Howard Avenue lists 309) men present and ready for duty. According to Hassler, in *Crisis at the Cross Roads: The First Day at Gettysburg*, the 61st arrived about 1 P.M. and reinforced the 45th New York.

One veteran of Company A described the 61st's arrival as follows, "on the 30th of June we found ourselves at Emetsburg and 1 July there came marching orders. When we had marched about 3 miles we could hear canons and then commenced to double quick to the battlefield. We got there and deployed skirmishers and our Corps went to fighting."

The plaque commemorating the Army of the Potomac, XI Corps, 3rd Division, 1st Brigade reads:

> Brig. Gen. Alex. Schimmelfennig, Col. George Von Amsberg 82d Illinois, 45th, 157th New York, 61st Ohio, 74th Pennsylvania Infantry. July 1 Arrived about 1 P.M. and advanced to connect with the right

Monument to 61st Ohio
Gettysburg, Pennsylvania

Photo by Robert G. Carroon

Base of Monument to 61st Ohio
Gettysburg, Pennsylvania

Photo by Robert G. Carroon

of First Corps on Oak Hill but was met by Heavy artillery and musketry fire and after being engaged between two and three hours and pressed closely upon the front and flanks by superior numbers the Brigade was compelled to retire with the Corps at 4 P.M. through the town to Cemetery Hill. The streets and alleys of the town became congested with the mass of infantry and artillery and many were captured. The Brigade formed and took position on Cemetery Hill between the First and Second Divisions of the Corps. July 2. At 4 P.M. the Brigade was subjected to a heavy artillery fire converging on Cemetery Hill. At dark a sudden attack was made on the right and the Brigade was sent to the support of Brig. Gen. A. Ames and returned after midnight except the 74th Pennsylvania which remained under the command of Brig. Gen. A. Ames. July 3. Skirmishing, not engaged.

The 61st, together with the 74th Pennsylvania, engaged the Confederate force of Georgians, commanded by Brigadier General George Dole which were part of Major General Robert E. Rodes's Division. The 61st was on the extreme right of the 1st Brigade commanded by Colonel George von Amsberg and so was next to the 82nd Ohio of the 2nd Brigade under Colonel Waldimir Krzyzanowski. By 2:00 P.M. the deployment of the two divisions under Major General Carl Schurz was completed. The action which followed resulted in the defeat of the XI Corps which was forced to retreat through the town of Gettysburg and take up a position on Cemetery Hill.

The marker to the 61st describes the action as follows:

On arriving from Emmittsburg about one o'clock P.M., July 1st 1863 was deployed as a skirmish line in advance of its brigade and moved towards Oak Hill. Later it supported a section of Dilger's Battery and engaged the enemy on this ground. After an obstinate contest it withdrew with the 11th Corps to Cemetery Hill. On the evening of July 2d it moved to the assistance of the 12th Corps on Culps Hill and returning lay on Cemetery Hill during the remainder of the battle.

The 61st was part of the general withdrawal of elements of the I and XI Corps through the town of Gettysburg which movement became a very disorganized retreat by the time the regiment reached the divisional rallying point just inside the cemetery gate house. Colonel Edward S. Salomon of the 82nd Illinois, in an address before the California Commandery of the Military Order of the Loyal Legion in 1912, stated, "...my regiment, being the center of the whole line, was the last to leave the field. I received orders to cover our retreat through the town with my own regiment, the 82nd Illinois and the 61st Ohio. These two regiments, under my command, were the last to enter the town in which the greatest confusion reigned."

If a sign of flight for a military unit is gaged by the amount of equipment it discards during the retreat then the 61st retired in good order for at Weaversville, Virginia, on September 1, 1863, when the quarter master issued supplies for the first time following the battle he only had to provide 8 knapsacks, 6 haversacks, 3 canteens, and 1 shelter tent. So the indication is that despite those killed, wounded, or taken prisoner the 61st was in good order when it took its position inside the gate near Dilger's Battery. The right and left flank markers of the 61st are prominent with their XI Corps crescent badge alongside the road into the cemetery.

In the action during the first day at Gettysburg the 61st took 54 casualties. Among the dead at the end of the action were Assistant Surgeon William S. Moore, Captain James M. Reynolds of Company B and Lieutenant Daniel W. Williams of Company G. Three officers, Lieutenant Edmund V. Brent of Company D, Lieutenant Daniel O. Sullivan of Company K, and Captain Frederick S. Wallace of Company A were wounded. Captain Henry R. Bending of Company I and Lieutenant Joseph R. P. Mell of Company F were captured and remained in Confederate prison camps until the end of the war.

The 61st Ohio was involved in the night action surrounding Cemetery Hill. Major General Carl Schurz, in a report to Major General Howard on August 20, 1863, wrote that "Of the part taken by my Division in the actions of July 2 and 3 at Gettysburg, I have the honor to submit the following report: One of the five regiments of the 1st Brigade, the 74th Pennsylvania, was left with General Ames to strengthen his right wing; the remaining four were directed towards a strip of woods on the right of the Division, in which the firing had become very heavy, and where, according to a report of some of the staff officers of the 1st Corps, immediate aid was needed. Two regiments, the 157th New York and the 61st Ohio were guided by one of their officers, while the other two, the 82nd Illinois and the 45th New York were led by my Chief of Staff, Lieutenant-Colonel Otto, of the 50th New York. It had meanwhile become quite dark, the direction of the fight being indicated by nothing but the sound of musketry. The regiment entered the woods with the greatest determination and drove the enemy from our rifle pits."

The 61st Ohio held its position on Cemetery Hill until the close of battle on July 3, 1863, and witnessed Pickett's Charge from that position. On July 5 the regiment joined in pursuit of the retreating Confederates and on July 12 skirmished with a portion of the rearguard of Lee's army near Hagerstown, Maryland.

The first formal regimental morning report issued after Gettysburg was that written at Weaversville, Virginia on August 29. In the report Colonel McGroarty listed present for duty 15 field, staff and company officers and 198 enlisted men for a total of 213. Assigned to special duty were 1 commissioned officer and 60 enlisted men, and 7 commissioned officers and 101 enlisted men were sick. Six enlisted men were under arrest or confinement. On detached service within the department were 2 commissioned officers and 41 enlisted men, and 3 commissioned officers were on detached service out of the department. One commissioned officer and 3 enlisted men were absent on leave. AWOL were 1 commissioned officer and 8 enlisted men which gave the 61st Ohio after the Battle of Gettysburg 30 commissioned officers and 417 enlisted men for an aggregate of 447. McGroarty also felt it necessary to report that "Corpl. [Jacob] Leifer, Co. 'E', 1st Sgt. [Henry] Bevard, Co. 'E', Sgt. Maj. [Marcus] Leifer, Co. 'E' and Corpl. [Amos] Daily, Co. 'K' were captured and irregularly paroled at Gettysburg, Pa. They were kept in a camp somewhere in Pa. until it was broken up." Apparently the men then simply went home to Columbus, Ohio without reporting to their regiment. They all later returned.

From July 26 to September 25 the regiment guarded the Orange and Alexandria Railroad from incursions of Confederate cavalry. On September 26 it, with other units of the XI Corps, was transported to the Army of the Cumberland, along with the XII Corps, reaching Bridgeport, Alabama, on October 1, 1863. Private Thaddeus K. Miller in a letter to his father noted that some of the regiment received furloughs at that time but most did not.

On October 27 the regiment started for Chattanooga, Tennessee, to aid in opening communications by way of the Tennessee River, with that beleaguered city. On the night of October 28 it was engaged in a fierce fight at Wauhatchie Valley, defeating and driving the Confederate forces across Lookout Creek. In this fight Captain William McGroarty of Company G, brother of the colonel of the regiment, and two others were killed and a number wounded.

On November 22 the 61st crossed the Tennessee River and marched to Chattanooga, Tennessee, where it joined the main army. On November 23, 24, and 25 the regiment was engaged in the fight at Missionary Ridge, moving around on the third day to the extreme left of the Union lines, to prevent a flanking movement on the part of the enemy.

Four days later the Ohioans joined with other elements of the Union forces in marching to the relief of Knoxville. Reaching a point within ten miles of Knoxville, the 61st received orders to return to Chattanooga. The regiment stopped and went into winter quarters in Wauhatchie Valley, but did not remain at this point over two weeks. It then returned to Bridgeport, Alabama, and there went into winter quarters.

Introduction

In February 1864, the officers and men were asked to re-enlist for the remainder of the war. On February 21, 262 men re-enlisted and on February 25, 21 commissioned officers re-enlisted. This was a sufficient number for the regiment to receive its "Veteran" status and be furloughed home to Ohio for sixty days. Major Bown applied for transportation for 22 line and staff officers, 262 enlisted men, 6 servants, 11 horses and the regimental baggage, and the 61st went home for the first time since it marched out of Camp Chase in 1862. On April 28, 1864, the regiment re-assembled at Camp Dennison, Ohio, and on the same day started for the front, reaching Chattanooga on May 5. It joined the main force of the Union army at Rocky Face Ridge (Trickum Post Office, Georgia on the East Chickamauga) on May 7. This was the commencement of the Atlanta Campaign. In this campaign the 61st was brigaded with the 3rd Brigade, 1st Division, XX Army Corps (which had been created by a merger of the XI and XII Corps) under the command of Major General Joseph Hooker. Their brigade commander was Colonel James S. Robinson of the 82nd Ohio. Marching from Rocky Face Ridge through Snake Creek Gap to the vicinity of Resaca, Georgia, the regiment, on May 14, was ordered to aid General Howard in preventing a flanking movement of the enemy on his left. On the evening of that day the 61st had an engagement with the enemy, in which it drove them and rescued the 5th Indiana Battery which was about to be overrun and which had been abandoned by its support. Several men were wounded in this affair.

Colonel Robinson described the action as follows: "On the farther side of the valley was another thickly wooded hill, and upon a slight knoll in the open field at our feet stood the Fifth Indiana Battery, supported by a portion of Stanley's division of the Fourth Corps. The division itself was at that time engaging the enemy some distance beyond the farther end of the valley, and from the character of the firing it was evident that General Stanley's lines were falling back; in fact that they were giving way in some disorder. By direction of General Williams I immediately formed my brigade in line of battle along the crest of the ridge parallel to and overlooking the valley. I had four regiments in front and two in the rear, thus forming two lines, one in support of the other. In my first line were the One hundred and first Illinois, Eighty-second Illinois, and the One hundred and forty-third and Forty-fifth New York Volunteers and in the second the Sixty-first and Eighty Second Ohio Volunteers. I had hardly gotten my command into position when the enemy swarmed out of the woods in pursuit of Stanley's men, and with defiant yells made for the battery, when I was directed by the brigadier-general commanding division to precipitate my entire command into the valley, and wheeling it upon the right flank, bring it up to the support of the battery. This order was at once communicated to the regiments of my brigade, and in a moment the whole was in motion. The evolution was executed with enthusiasim and with no less precision and regularity of movement than might have been expected upon drill. Arriving at the front of the battery the Eighty-second Illinois, Sixty-first Ohio, and One hundred and forty-third New York Volunteers poured a tremendous fire upon the overconfident foe....the enemy at once gave way and confusedly sought his entrenchments back in the woods."

May 15 saw the 61st participate in the bloody battle of Resaca, where they lost several men. In the afternoon they assisted in repulsing a heavy attack made by the enemy on their left flank with the intent of gaining the Dalton road. The retreating Confederates were pursued for two or three days as they fled toward the Allatoona Mountain. On May 19 the 61st caught up with the enemy and drove them about two miles to Cassville, Georgia. The regiment then went into camp and remained there until May 23. On that day it crossed the Etowah River and the Allatoona Mountain and resumed the march. On May 25 the army again found the enemy near Dallas, Georgia. At this point the 61st, then occupying the extreme rear of the 1st Division, was ordered to the front of the division and deployed as skirmishers. The 61st drove the enemy's skirmish line for some distance and advanced on their rifle pits. While engaged in this duty the regiment lost six men killed and seventeen wounded.

On May 28, the regiment was ordered to return to Kingston to guard an ammunition train, and did not again reach the main army until May 31. On June 1 it moved around to the left of the IV Corps, which position it retained until June 2. During this time the soldiers were frequently engaged with the enemy.

On June 3, the regiment moved further to the left and skirmished with the enemy. These flanking movements were continued up to June 15 when the regiment had reached the vicinity of Lost Mountain. On the morning of June 16 five men were wounded while lying behind temporary breastworks.

On June 17, the enemy was driven and skirmished with and on June 19 and 21 the regiment reached and moved around the base of Kennesaw Mountain. On June 22, it moved up still further and built works at Kolb's Farm. While building these works the enemy made a dash on the Union lines, and for a few minutes had things all their own way, but the troops rallied and drove them back. Major David C. Beckett was killed, and one officer, Lieutenant William A. Smith, and six men were wounded. Private David Fishel of the 61st described the action in a letter of June 26, 1864: "We are lying here behind very strong breastworks looking the Johnnies right in the eyes. We have a heavy skirmish line [in] front of us; they keep firing day and night. The

Rebs hold the Kenesaw mountain yet our men are placing some heavy pieces in position to scare them off. We had a brisk fight on the 22nd. We lost our major, D.C. Beckett. You will see a notice in the Cincinnati papers of what we soldiers thought of him. We had one man shot dead yesterday in relieving the pickets. The Rebs take all advantage of this sort. Last night our picket boys called out to the Reb pickets to come over and see Joe Hooker and get a Cracker. They said Hooker was not there he could not be everywhere. Yes Johnny come over Hooker is not one mile from here. They dread Hooker worse than we did Stonewall Jackson...We are three miles from Marietta south on the pike. The Rebs don't want to go to Marietta for fear we will burn the place. They are on the last range of hills [and] our cavalry are on the flat ground between here and Marietta...we have 23 pieces of artillery where our breastwork crosses the pike all masked. On the east of the pike is a swamp a man can scarcely walk through..."

While this fight was in progress a serious incident occurred. Colonel McGroarty was ordered to advance his regiment to a certain point, but in executing the order he placed it far beyond the line intended, and in the dark became almost isolated from his brigade. An attempt was made by a Confederate regiment to capture them; but in moving through the dense woods in the dark the men of the Confederate regiment were detached from their officers, and becoming alarmed, attempted to hide themselves in the thickets. The 61st, in falling back to its proper line, stumbled across these fellows and captured a large number of them. Colonel McGroarty, with his own hands, brought in seventeen of the frightened Confederates.

The Chattahoochie River was crossed at four o'clock in the afternoon of June 17 and the regiment went into camp on its banks. June 18 and 19 were consumed in marching to Peachtree Creek. On July 20 the regiment crossed Peachtree Creek and skirmished with the enemy until four o'clock in the afternoon, when the Confederates made a desperate attempt to drive the Union forces back across the Chattahoochie. The fight was one of the most desperate of the war in which the 61st was engaged. The 61st was part of Brigadier General James Sydney Robinson's Brigade which, together with that commanded by Brigadier General Joseph Farmer Kniepe, was assaulted in a densely wooded area by Major General Edward Cary Walthall's Division. The 61st received a devastating volley at point blank range and were flanked on both left and right. They fell back and regrouped, aided by other elements of Major General Alpheus Starkey Williams's Division.

For a moment Confederates were in full tide of success, but the XX Corps, under Major General Hooker stood firm and drove them back to their main works. In the Battle of Peachtree Creek five officers, including Colonel McGroarty, were wounded and one killed. Over seventy of the other ranks were wounded and eighteen or twenty killed. Together with Gettysburg it proved to be the most devastating fight in which the 61st was engaged as far as the number of serious casualties is concerned. At the end of the action the regiment could report only 14 commissioned officers and 194 enlisted men for an aggregate of 208 with 194 guns and 11,640 rounds of ammunition as well as "Axes 3."

On July 27 the regiment and corps were sent back to the Chattahoochie to guard the bridge. The 61st remained in the rear until August 5 when, with the capture of Atlanta, the corps moved up and went into camp on the east side of the city.

The regiment lay at Atlanta until November 15, when it started with General William Tecumseh Sherman's army on its "march to the sea." In this great march the regiment had but one skirmish with the enemy—at Sandersonville, Georgia.

While lying at Savannah the 61st was detached from its brigade and assigned to a Provisional Brigade, on duty in the city. About the middle of January 1865, it moved with the 2nd Brigade of the XX Corps, under General John White Geary, to Sister's Ferry, on the Savannah River. Crossing the river, after a week's detention, it marched to the vicinity of Robertsville, South Carolina, and there joined its proper command.

Aside from hard marches through the swamps of South Carolina nothing of interest occurred until Bentonville, North Carolina, was reached. At this point the last real battle of the march was fought. The 61st Ohio performed its part in this battle, and lost some men wounded and captured.

Marching with the army the regiment reached Goldsboro, North Carolina, and there went into camp. Here the 61st was consolidated with the 82nd Ohio, the combined regiment taking the name of the latter-named organization.

This act blotted from the rolls of the army the name of the 61st Ohio, but its deeds remain on record. The 61st's losses by the casualties on the field were so numerous that at the close of its service a little band of only about sixty officers and men remained to answer to the last roll call.

The consolidated regiment, now the 82nd Ohio, marched through Richmond to Washington, D.C., where it participated in the Grand Review, was sent home to Columbus, Ohio, and there mustered out of the service on or about September 1, 1865.

Capt. Frederick Stephens Wallace, Company A,
61st Ohio Volunteer Infantry

Seward R. Osborne Collection, USAMHI

The Sixty-First Ohio Volunteers
1861-1865

By Frederick Stephens Wallace
Formerly Captain 61st Ohio Volunteers
Late Major 82nd Ohio Volunteers

(First published as a privately printed booklet for the Regimental Association of the 61st and 82nd Ohio Veteran Volunteer Infantry in 1902)

Note

Preceding the account by Frederick Stephens Wallace

This sketch, which was originally written at the solicitation of Comrade Jewett, President of the Association of the 61st and 82nd Ohio Veteran Volunteer Infantry, to be read at the annual reunion at Cleveland, Ohio on September 12, 1901, was intended to be merely a narrative of some of the prominent events occurring in the history of the 61st, and the writer supposed that the reading of it would be the ending of it. It was so well received, however, and the desire to have it put in a more permanent form was so unanimous, that the writer has added to it—or rather interjected—some historical matter, with the view of making it of real value to those for whose benefit it was written. In collecting these facts the aid of Comrades Miller, Jewett, Schultz, Harris, and Mullen is gratefully acknowledged.

The most valuable heritage a man, and especially a soldier, can leave to his descendants is a good name, and if this sketch will have the effect of aiding to impress on the minds of those into whose hands it may fall a correct idea of the "Man of 1861–1865" and of the part they took in the successful efforts to preserve this great Nation to posterity, the writer will be more than satisfied.

Chattanooga, Tenn. August 1902
The Sixty-First Ohio Volunteer Infantry

Responding to the call of President Lincoln immediately following the reverse to the Union Army at Bull Run, Va., in July, 1861, the enlisting of volunteers "for the war" was actively prosecuted throughout the loyal states. Never before was there such a universal response to the demands of a nation in its hour of peril; and flocking to the various rendezvous came the young manhood of the country. In those days there was no thought of bounty. Patriotism animated each breast and recruits came pouring in.

Among the organizations authorized by the government of the State of Ohio were the Fiftieth Regiment of Infantry, under Colonel Stephen J. McGroarty, to assemble at Hamilton, Ohio, the Fifty-second Regiment, under Colonel Charles Sargent, to assemble at Camp Dennison, Ohio, and the Sixty-first Regiment, under Colonel Newton W. Schleich, to assemble at Lancaster, O. Quickly was each one of these regiments recruited up to near the 1,020 required for a full command, only to be depleted more than once by the detaching of whole companies to fill gaps occasioned by losses in the regiments in the field. Chafing at being held in the rear while their comrades were on the fighting line, the demands of those who remained at last had the effect of causing the governor to send them to the front, without waiting to again fill up the ranks. The preparatory step was the consolidating of the three regiments into one, and thus the Sixty-first was created. The original field and staff was as follows: Newton W. Schleich, of the Sixty-first, Colonel; Stephen J. McGroarty, of the Fiftieth, Lieutenant Colonel; W. H. H. Bown, of the Fifty-second, Major; Leonidas M. Jewett, Adjutant; Enoch Pearce, Surgeon; Wm. S. Moore, Assistant Surgeon; George W. Wygram, Quartermaster, and Edward P. Corcoran, Chaplain.

Composed of natives of nearly every county in the state, together with a sprinkling of foreign born, liberty-loving citizens, embracing men of various religious beliefs—the Protestant, the Catholic and the Hebrew; containing in the ranks the clerk from the city and the farmer lad; the professional man, the laborer, the mechanic, the merchant and the student, all combined to create in the Sixty-first Ohio a typical regiment of American volunteers. To give its full history, with all the details, would require a volume; what follows is mainly a sketch of its itinerancy. Generally the dates are correct and in this fact lies its value, aside from such interest as the narrative portion may possess for the members of the regiment and their families.

The skeleton regiments assembled at Camp Chase near Columbus, Ohio, when the consolidation into the Sixty-first was effected April 23, 1862, a large surplus being left over at the nucleus of a new organization.

The regiment remained at Camp Chase, drilling and receiving its equipment, until May 27, 1862, on which date it started by rail for the front, reaching New Creek, West Virginia, on the 28th. Here the real campaigning began, the command marching for Romney, Virginia, on the 29th, leaving the baggage train to follow. From Romney marched to Moorefield, Virginia, and remained a few days. While lying there a portion of the regiment, under Lieut. Col. McGroarty, was ordered to hurry to Little Petersburg, some miles distant, to protect some wounded men and some supplies left by Fremont's forces. Responding to the alarm of the long roll, sounded in the middle of the night, the command was formed and the march began in the intense darkness. Reaching there the next day, after wading the north branch of the Potomac, among the very few occupants found there, besides those in the hospital was Sutler Spitzer, of the Fifty fifth Ohio, whose tent was on the line selected by Colonel McGroarty for the location of the regiment with the view of repelling a possible attack. It coming to the ears of the men that the sutler was not moving out of the way with the alacrity desired by the Colonel, they voluntarily assisted him, with the result that when he came to reassemble his stores many of them, his stock of limburger cheese excepted, were missing. Search by the officers failed to locate the goods and not until forty years afterwards did Comrade Mullen confess that he and his intimates, Schultz, Gilchrist and Harris, were playing a game of cards on the blanket covering a buried box of the plunder while the tent was being searched. So early do some soldiers become accomplished veterans! In the end the sutler was paid by assessment on the officers, and no such breach of discipline ever afterwards occurred.

Returning to Moorefield from Little Petersburg, the regiment lay there a few days and then marched to Strasburg, Virginia, arriving June 23, 1862, and joining Fremont's forces there. Up to this time the regiment had been an independent command and its march through a country lately held by the enemy and still infested by his bushwhackers and small bodies of irregular troops, required the exercise of the greatest caution to prevent surprise, and was not without its excitements.

From Strasburg they marched to Middletown, Virginia, arriving June 29, 1862, and remaining some two weeks. Here, if memory is correct, the Eighth Virginia, Seventy-fourth Pennsylvania and Sixty-first Ohio regiments were brigaded. Later the Eighth Virginia was sent to Milroy's command and the Forty-fifth New York took its place. Drilling in brigade and corps formation began here and was a daily thing, from dawn until dark, under the direction, mostly, of skilled officers educated in the best military schools of Europe, many of whom held high positions in the armies of Germany and France, but who now nobly gave their services to the cause of liberty.

The next move was through Luray Court House to Port Royal, Virginia, and thence across the Blue Ridge to Sperryville, Virginia, arriving about the middle of July 1862. The regiment lay here with the other troops nearly a month, during which time the incessant drilling was kept up, with the result that the entire command was now a splendid body of well trained soldiers.

From Sperryville the troops were hurried to the support of Major General Nathaniel P. Banks, who was coping with Stonewall Jackson, reaching Cedar Mountain late in the day while the fight was still going on, and going into line of battle but not becoming engaged. During the night the enemy withdrew and the Sixty-first did not have an opportunity to show its fighting qualities here. This was on August 9, 1862.

On August 16, 1862, the campaign of General John Pope which ended with the Second Battle of Bull Run began. For several days the regiment was among the troops guarding the fords of the Rappahannock against any attempt the enemy might make to cross the river, being at Kelly's Ford on August 18th, at White Sulpher Springs on the 21st and at Freeman's Ford on the 22nd, when the Sixty-first had its first real engagement during a reconnaissance to the south side of the river by the brigade. The survivors doubtless recall the wading of the river, waist deep, by an intricate ford: the advance of the line, preceded by the skirmishers to the top of the ridge; the fierce fighting there and the holding of the ground until both flanks were enveloped—a division of the enemy against a brigade. Then came the falling back, firing and in good order as far as the Sixty-first was concerned until the river was reached and the recrossing under the fire from Dilger's Battery which effectively checked the enemy's advance—a service which the Sixty-first repaid more than once afterwards. No troops could have behaved better than did the men of the Sixty-first in this affair, and with a few notable exceptions the conduct of every man was creditable. The loss in killed and wounded was heavy, the number not now being remembered. It was here, also, that the brave General Henry Bohlen was killed right on the firing line. Immediately following this battle the command of the regiment devolved on Lieutenant Colonel McGroarty and soon afterwards he was promoted to Colonel. Major Bown to Lieutenant Colonel and Captain Beckett to Major.

On August 23rd and 24th the command was again at Sulpher Springs, where the Sixty-first had the nerve-shaking experience of lying for hours in an open field under the enemy's artillery fire without opportunity of replying. Not one of the shells exploded during the entire cannonading, which accounts for the regiment's escaping without casualty. On August 25, 1862, occurred the affair at Waterloo Bridge where, under cover of continuous volleys by the other regiments, the gallant Eighty-second Ohio destroyed the bridge. On August 28th the regiment was at Gainesville, Virginia, on the 29th at Groveton, and on that day and the 30th occurred the second Bull Run battle. This being the first great engagement in which the regiment participated, particulars as to the part taken by it will be of interest.

At daylight on the morning of August 30, 1862, the Sixty-first was ordered to develop the enemy's position in its front. Three companies under command of the writer, detailed for that purpose by Adjutant Leonidas M. Jewett, then the enthusiastic young officer of volunteers, now the dignified and portly judge—the honored president of your association—formed the advance. Deployed as skirmishers they moved rapidly but cautiously to the front through the wooded country, sending to the rear scores of the enemy's stragglers who surrendered without resistance, until, probably a mile from the starting point, the line suddenly brought up against a battery which opened on it with grape and canister at short range. While holding the ground under this fire orders were brought by a staff officer for the skirmishers to rejoin the regiment now moving in another direction, and after an hour's march this was effected just in time to be in the thick of the fight at the railroad. For some hours the line of which it formed a part was in the front of battle, now attacking, now repelling attack; giving and receiving volley after volley until the cartridge boxes were emptied, then relieved by fresh troops for a time; then, with cartridge boxes refilled, to the front again and more fighting; then two or three changes of position, and finally at night the regiment, depleted by many casualties, posted at the stone bridge to cover the crossing of the troops. Such is the history of the regiment's part on that day as recalled after the lapse of nearly forty years. Although victory was not with us here it was not the fault of the rank and file of the army nor yet of General Pope, whose splendid generalship was nullified by the incompetency, or worse, of a corps commander who although on the field of battle failed to put his men into action at all, although having full knowledge of what might result from such failure.

Let me digress and recall a circumstance which always comes to my mind in thinking of this battle and which some of you may remember. When the regiment took its position at the bridge that dark night, tired, hungry and depressed, in silence so as not to draw the fire of the nearby enemy, it was its fortune to halt along the camp mess of some troops who had been driven from their position just before nightfall by the enemy's shells, which even yet occasionally came shrieking by unpleasantly near. Hanging on a pole over some still smoldering embers were half a dozen kettles of soup, while lying around were several boxes of hardtack and sides of bacon. Ye gods! what a feast for men who had not had a real meal for weeks! Silently the soup was ladled into the "blenkers," silently the hardtack was divided out, silently the bacon was sliced, then for a time there were sounds of the sipping of soup and the crunching of crackers. As for the bacon, raw it was found and raw it was devoured. To one at least whose haversack with servant attachment had been missing a couple of days no banquet before or since has brought the enjoyment given by that "snack" in the darkness at the stone bridge.

About midnight, the last of the troops having passed, the Sixty-first crossed over and the bridge was destroyed; and the writer, who thirteen months before had led a detachment of pioneers of the First and Second Ohio regiments over the bridge in the advance of the Union army, had the honor on this occasion of being with the rear guard.

As the marches of a regiment, as well as its battles, form part of its history, it may not be out of place to describe briefly that from Sperryville to Bull Run, as a type of many that followed, only that some were through the snow and others through the rain and mud, all accompanied by hardships that seem almost unbearable. On this campaign the movements of the commissary trains were erratic from the start. Some fell prey to the enemy, while those that escaped did not show themselves for days at a time. The result was hunger for the soldier. Fortunately, there were cornfields and bees, and many a meal was made from green corn with honey dessert. It was not uncommon sight to see a soldier "streaking it" across a field with a beehive on his shoulder, the open end to the rear. Then there was the plague of the red dust, ground to an impalpable powder by the feet and wheels of a never resting army, saturating the clothing and penetrating to the skin of the perspiring soldier, breathed into his lungs in suffocating quantity, caking in his mouth and creating a thirst not quenchable by the tepid water of the canteen. Who of you does not recall the struggle with the crowd at the infrequent well, to be rewarded after a long wait by a swallow of muddy dregs, grateful only by reason of its coolness? As to the baggage trains, they were not visible more than once, if at all, during the entire campaign, and the insect horror, due to inability to procure change of clothing, is only to be hinted at. Then there was the bivouacking in the rain; the worn out shoes; the dysentery; the weakness of poorly nourished men; the sweltering heat of the dog days. Yet, at the end of such a march, the men were ready and anxious to meet the foe. They fought a good fight, and if not victorious it was not the fault of the men in the ranks.

On September 2, 1862, the regiment was at Chantilly, Virginia, with the troops engaged in the night fight when General Philip Kearny was killed. From here, as part of the rear guard, it marched to the defenses of Washington, and as part of the First Brigade (Schimmelfennig), Third Division (Schurz), Eleventh Corps (Sigel), it formed part of the grand reserve, stationed most of the time in the vicinity of the Chain Bridge. On November 2, occurred the reconnaissance in force to Throughfare Gap, and thence to Centerville. On December 10 to 15, the

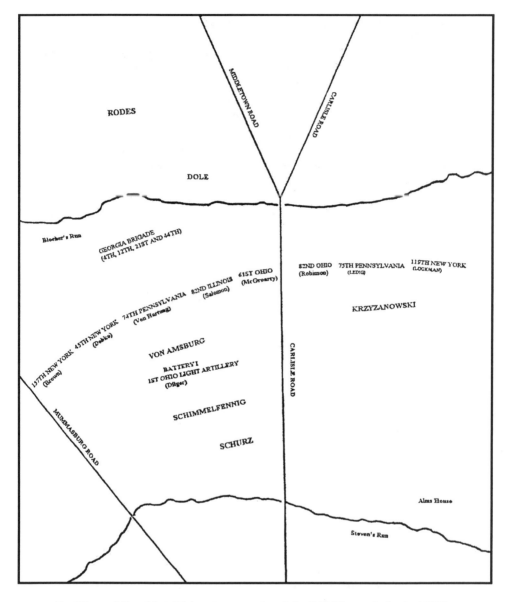

Position of the 61st Ohio at approximately 2 P.M. on July 1, 1863
Map by Robert G. Carroon

regiment participated in Burnside's Fredericksburg campaign, but did not take part in the fighting. After a short stay at Falmouth, Virginia, the regiment moved to Acquia Creek, Virginia, and went into winter quarters, remaining until January 20, 1863. On that day marched to near Hartwood Church and built winter quarters, which it occupied just one day. Then came the never-to-be-forgotten "Mud March" continuing night and day in a pouring rain until January 24. Again built winter quarters, this time at Stafford Court House, and remained there until April 27, 1863. On this date the campaign which ended at Chancellorsville began, the Eleventh Corps crossing the Rappahannock at Kelly's Ford, and taking the position assigned to it south of the river, with an interval of a mile of broken, wooded country between it and the nearest corps.

On May 2, 1863, the Sixty-first, with the other regiments of Schurz's division, lay for hours in line of battle, stretched along a narrow road, walled in by dense woods front and rear, facing to the south and prepared for an attack from that direction. On the right of Schurz, and forming the right of the line, lay Brigadier General Charles Nathaniel Devens' (formerly McLean's) division of true and tried soldiers, also mostly stretched along the road and facing south. But it was not characteristic of Stonewall Jackson to attack where he was expected to, and this fact was well known to every man in the corps, excepting, apparently General Devens and General Howard. During these hours of waiting by the Federals, Jackson was moving to Howard's right and rear with the full knowledge of these two officers, conveyed to them more than once from most trustworthy sources, and still no move was made to meet the impending attack. Deliberately, in sight of Federal pickets and within musket shot of some parts of the Federal lines, Jackson deployed his lines and massed his reserves, and still no move by Howard.

Suddenly, just as the day of the second was closing, the enemy's shells came pouring in on the unprotected flank and rear of the corps, followed by an infantry charge so sudden that the Federals, while attempting to change front on ground covered with dense woods and filled with undergrowth, interlaced with rope-like vines of the greenbriar and wild grape, found the enemy upon and among them. Thrown into confusion, Devens' men, who received the first shock, fell back, mainly along the narrow road, all the time under a galling fire, which they were unable to return, and carried with them for perhaps a quarter of a mile, those regiments of Schurz's division which were in line along the road, wholly unable to extricate themselves until clear of the woods. All this occurred in a very few minutes.

As soon as the somewhat open country was reached attempts to form a line across the enemy's advance were made, with fair success from the very start, and resistance began, which became more effective as the men singly and in squads succeeded in finding their commands. This resistance was kept up into the night, every point of vantage being used to check the enemy.

The spontaneity with which the men rallied after the first shock gives the lie to those traducers of the Eleventh Corps (and this includes its commander), who sought a scapegoat on which to unload the burden of their own sins and shortcomings and blundering. So anxious were the men, whose commands had been scattered, to help retrieve the disaster, that they gladly attached themselves to any body of troops showing formation, each man actuated by his own soldierly instinct, and being not at all affected by General Howard's theatrical manner, as he shouted, waving his pistol with his only hand, "Rally! men, Rally! or I am ruined!" His exhibition of personal courage was creditable, but the most humble volunteer had scant respect for the man who they knew was responsible for the disaster. As an example of the spirit of the men, some two or three hundred of whom attached themselves to the writer's company, not one of them wavered under fire, nor fell back without orders. Each one had retained his gun, his ammunition and his blanket. Soldiers who are demoralized rid themselves of such impediments at the start, and such is the difference between brave men thrown into confusion and those who, coward-like, run from danger.

In the melee at the beginning the Sixty-first was badly broken. A movement to change front had just begun when Devens' men came pouring through the line. To maintain organization under such pressure was out of the question; but although the regiment was broken into three fragments the fragments themselves cohered, and all were reunited later. Our portion found itself north of the road and rendered good service in fighting with the troops there, as is shown by the official reports. Another portion was south of the road, and formed part of a line of troops rallied from different commands, and which, although in irregular formation, fought well and offered stubborn resistance. A third portion kept along the road and was in support of Captain Hubert Dilger's battery until the battle ended. Among those who helped serve the guns the names of Comrades Mackey, Spellman, Schultz and Kirtz are recalled.

As to the general reputation of the regiment, and particularly as to the part it took in the Battle of Chancellorsville, the following quotations are of value, coming as they do from one who was in no way connected with it.

They are taken from a volume entitled "The Battle of Chancellorsville," written by Augustus Choate Hamilin, formerly Lieutenant Colonel and Medical Inspector, U.S. Army, published by the author at Bangor, Maine, 1896. He says (p. 40): "Among the veteran regiments there were six from the State of Ohio, nearly all American citizens, and equal in courage, intelligence and patriotism to any in the armies of the United States. Their reputation had been fully established long before the Battle of Chancellorsville, in the campaigns of Western Virginia and at Cross Keys, and in the second Manassas, where most of them won special praise. They were the Twenty-fifth, the Fifty-fifth, the Sixty-first, the Seventy-third, the Seventy-fifth, and the Eighty-second, all of which were commanded by American officers of acknowledged ability and courage. No words of praise are necessary for Col. Richardson, of the Twenty-fifth; for Col. John C. Lee, of the Fifty-fifth; for Col. Stephen J. McGroarty, of the Sixty-first; for Col. Orland Smith of the Seventy-third; for Col. Robert Riley, of the Seventy-fifth, or for that noble man and officer, Col. James S. Robinson, of the Eighty-second Ohio Regiment.

"All of these regiments, excepting the Seventy-third, than attached with Barlow, were in the fight, and attempted to do their duty, and did do it, at a terrible sacrifice of their men, for which adequate praise has not been given. It would be difficult to find six trustier regiments in all the armies of the United States than these. The Sixty-first Ohio was commanded by that sterling Irishman, Colonel Stephen J. McGroarty, and his regiment seemed to be largely of Irishmen, or men of Irish descent, so strong was the individuality of the commander. No one ever questioned McGroarty's courage or ability, and at the close of the war he could have exclaimed with Marius, 'My wounds are proof of my ability.' The report of this gallant officer is not to be found, and its absence is a serious loss to the history of the fight around Dowdall's and at the Church. It is certain, however, that the brave officer who held his regiment as rear guard until midnight on the deserted field of the second Bull Run, did all that one man could do in averting disaster in the face of ruin, or what appeared to be ruin.

"The Sixty-first was drawn up in line, facing the west (south), waiting for the enemy, when the wrecks of Devens' division, rushing down the road to escape the withering fire of Jackson's men, over-ran them and destroyed their formation and carried part of it away in the crowd, which continued on towards the Chancellor House. Parts of the broken regiment joined the line by the Church, and later on fell back to the Bushbeck line and fought there. Two of the companies attached themselves to Dilger's battery and stuck to him in the retreat, and followed him to his position in the line of artillery at Fairview, where they remained until morning."

At another place (p. 70), he speaks of "the Sixty-first Ohio and Seventy-fourth Pennsylvania, which were regarded as among the best troops in the corps." Again (p. 73) he says: "Dilger kept one gun with him, as it was all he could use with advantage at the rifle pit, and this he planted in the middle of the road and opened a rapid fire to his front. While here he was supported by two companies of the brave Sixty-first

Ohio, who stuck to him in the retreat and remained with him also at Fairview all night, when he took part in the cannonade." Also, on page 76: "Dilger, with his single gun retreated in the road, keeping the enemy out of his front by his rapid discharges of canister and solid shot. The two companies of the brave Irishmen of the Sixty-first still supported him, and besides there were a number of officers of high rank, including both General Howard and General Schurz, who also wished to help the artillerymen, who composed the rear guard." And, on page 78: "Dilger's resolute action while retreating with his single gun, supported by the two companies of brave Irishmen of the Sixty-first Ohio, keeping the enemy at bay and the Plank Road free from active pursuit, forms one of the bright and pleasing episodes of the ill fated campaign, but which has not received, even at this late day, the least notice whatever." (At another place the author gives the loss of the regiment in killed and wounded as sixty—about one-sixth of those engaged—and of the corps as over 2,600.)

These be words of praise, indeed, and the author does not fail to do justice also to those other sterling regiments of the corps, which came from New York, Pennsylvania, Connecticut, Illinois, Wisconsin and Ohio, whether composed of Americans by birth or by adoption.

Much more could be written as to the causes which led to the defeat at Chancellorsville, amongst them being the substitution of Howard for that ever vigilant soldier, Sigel, and of Devens for that fire-tried, noble officer, McLean. But that would be outside the scope of this sketch. Enough has been said to show that the part taken by the Sixty-first was not without credit, and the world has long known on whom to place the blame for the wrecking of Hooker's brilliant plan.

On May 6, 1863, the command returned to Stafford Court House, where it remained without anything important occurring in its history until the following month, when, on June 12, 1863, as a part of the army marching parallel with Lee, it began a northward march, which ended with the Battle of Gettysburg, Pennsylvania.

At this, the most momentous battle of the war, the Sixty-first opened the fight in the skirmish on the evening of July 1, 1863. On July 2nd and 3rd the battle raged furiously, resulting in a glorious victory for the Union armies, but at a cost attested by the thousands of graves in the nearby National Cemetery. Of the members of the Sixty-first who laid down their lives there the writer recalls the names of Dr. Moore, Capt. Reynolds and Lieutenants Williams and McMains, which occurred before the writer left the field, disabled, on the evening of July 2nd. What the Sixty-first did afterwards is shown by the high praise in the reports of the commanding general, and the long list of dead and wounded shows that the regiment bore its full part in the fray.

After the battle the Sixty-first formed part of the column pursuing Lee, without anything noticeable occurring except a skirmish, July 12, near Hagerstown, Maryland. From July 26th to September 25th the regiment was on guard duty along the Orange and Alexandria railroad, and no stirring events occurred.

On September 26, 1863, with the Eleventh and Twelfth Corps, it began the long journey by rail to reinforce the Army of the Cumberland at Chattanooga, Tennessee. On this bloodless campaign the troops accommodated themselves to the kinds of vehicles the railroad companies were able to furnish—flat cars, box cars, cattle cars or passenger coaches—with some grumbling perhaps, but with no promise of mutiny, as was shown by some of the brothers-in-arms in a later war.

On October 1, 1863, the troops disembarked at Bridgeport, Alabama, 28 miles from Chattanooga, Tennessee, and remained there nearly a month. It was from this place, about October 18, that 300 men of the Sixty-first under command of Lieutenant Colonel Bown, made a raid across Sand Mountain, some 12 or 15 miles, to Trenton, Georgia, expecting to surprise a post of the enemy there. The place was captured without firing a shot, as the Confederates themselves were absent on a raid. However, an important capture was made in the person of one General Nathan Bedford Forrest's staff officers, who was carrying dispatches to General Joseph Wheeler. Besides important papers, there was found in his dispatch bag a U.S. regimental flag, with a card pinned to it bearing the following inscription, "Colors of the Fourth (I think that was the number) Tennessee Federal Regiment, captured at McMinnville, Tennessee, (such a date not now remembered). With compliments of General Forrest to General Wheeler." This flag the writer had the pleasure of turning over the corps commander on returning to Bridgeport.

On October 27, 1863, the troops left Bridgeport, Alabama, for Chattanooga, Tennessee, and on the night of the 28th occurred the fight in Lookout Valley, when brave Captain McGroarty, brother of the Colonel, was killed. His last words to the writer were, "Tell my folks in Cincinnati that I fell fighting for my country." There were several other casualties here.

In speaking of this affair, Major Theodore A. Mysenberg, in a paper read before the Missouri Commandery of the Loyal Legion in 1891, says, "I will quote the remark of General Thomas, than who there was no braver, truer and talented commander. Thomas says, commenting upon the night engagement preceding the Battle of Chattanooga: 'The bayonet charge of Howard's troops made up the side of a steep and difficult hill, over two hundred feet high, completely routing and driving the enemy from his barricades on its top, will rank with the most distinguished feats of arms of this war.'"

Communication with the troops hemmed up in Chattanooga, Tennessee, having been opened by this and allied movements, the corps went into camp at Lookout Valley, near Wauhatchie, Tennessee, a few miles from the city, and immediately constructed strong rifle pits. While lying here the enemy made it interesting by daily sending a few shells from the top of Lookout Mountain into the camps, without any disastrous effect, however. On November 22, 1863, a part of the troops from Wauhatchie Valley, including the Sixty-first, joined the main body in Chattanooga, and on the 23rd, 24th and 25th, under the leadership of General Ulysses S. Grant, was fought the battles of Lookout Mountain and Missionary Ridge, a portion of the corps being engaged in the assault on the mountain, and the balance, including the Sixty-first, in the Missionary Ridge battle. The regiment was with the troops which drove the enemy from his works at Orchard Knob, and afterwards, on the left of the line, engaged in repelling the enemy's attempt to crush Major General William T. Sherman's left flank, finally driving him off. At this place several hundred Confederate soldiers surrendered to the Sixty-first.

After the battle the Sixty-first was part of the troops which pursued the enemy to near Ringgold, Georgia, where its direction was changed toward Knoxville, Tennessee, forming part of a column sent to relieve General Ambrose Burnside, who was besieged there. Reaching a point a few miles from Knoxville it was learned that the enemy had withdrawn, and our column returned to Chattanooga.

This Knoxville campaign, although a short one, was not without its hardships. No supply train accompanied the column, and the troops subsisted precariously on what the country afforded. As for clothing the men had just what they stood in after stripping for the Battle of Missionary Ridge. The enemy had destroyed all bridges, and for crossing the larger streams bridges made of wagons gathered from the surrounding country, placed side by side with planks stretched from one wagon to an other were used. The fordable streams were waded, and it was a frequent thing for the troops to go into bivouac at night with dripping clothing after having just waded an ice-cold stream, waist deep. Long before reaching Chattanooga the shoes were worn out and many of the men had only rough moccasins, made of green hides of the cattle killed for food, to keep their bruised feet from the frozen ground.

For soldierly conduct in this campaign the Sixty-first was specially mentioned by General Hector Tyndale in Grand Orders.

Reaching its old quarters near Chattanooga on December 17, 1863, it remained there a short time, and then with the other troops removed to Bridgeport, Alabama, where it remained on duty until March. Here the men of the Sixty-first again showed their patriotism by veteranizing, a sufficient number re-enlisting to enable the regiment to retain its organization. In the latter part of March, soon after the return of the Eighty-second from its veteran furlough, the Sixty-first took its turn and proceeded to Ohio, where for a month the soldiers enjoyed the pleasures of civil life among relatives and friends.

Late in April, 1864, the regiment reassembled at Camp Dennison, Ohio, and on the 28th, reinforced by a large number of recruits, it started to the front again, reaching Chattanooga on May 5th, the day on which the Atlanta campaign began, and joining its comrades on the 7th on Pea Vine Creek, near Rocky Face Ridge, Georgia. It formed part of the Third Brigade, First Division, Twentieth Corps, this Corps having been formed by the consolidation of the Eleventh and Twelfth the month previous. The brigade was composed of the Sixty-first and Eighty-second Ohio, the One Hundred and Forty-third New York and the One Hundred and First Illinois. It was the Third Brigade of the First Division of the Twentieth Corps, Army of the Cumberland, and was commanded by Brigadier General J. S. Robinson, formerly Colonel of the Eighty-second Ohio.

On May 8th to 10th the corps lay near Trickum, Georgia, excepting that on the night of the 9th the First division moved to Snake Creek Gap. On May 12th they marched towards Resacca, Georgia, and on the 13th and 14th maneuvered around that place, it being well fortified and held by a strong force of the enemy. Up to this time there had been much marching and but little fighting so far as the First division was concerned.

On the 14th of May the division was hurried to the support of the Fourth Corps, part of which was being driven back. It was on this occasion that the Sixty-first by a gallant spontaneous charge saved the Fifth Indiana Battery from capture.

On May 15th, 1864, the sanguinary battle of Resacca, Georgia, occurred. The Third Brigade (Robinson's) of which the Sixty-first formed part, occupied the extreme left of the Federal line, and the enemy made desperate efforts to turn that flank. Three times against its unprotected front their double lines charged with the utmost determination, and three times were they repulsed by the unflinching Federals, finally retreating before a determined charge by the brigade and leaving the ground covered with their dead from within a few yards of the First division's front back to the railroad, a thousand yards distant. In this charge the Sixty-first captured the colors of a Confederate regiment.

From Resacca the beaten enemy retreated southwardly, the Union troops pursuing, and on the 17th the corps was south of the Oostenaula River, camping that night near Calhoun. On May 19th the enemy was struck again near Cassville, Georgia, but after a sharp skirmish, in which the Sixty-first participated, he evacuated his strong works there.

And here let it be noted that at a dozen strategic points between Chattanooga and Atlanta the enemy had the advantage of strong earthworks, some of them apparently having been constructed some time before they were occupied.

The command lay at Cassville three days, and on May 23rd resumed its march, crossing the Etowah River and going into position on the south side, near Stilesboro. On May 24th the regiment marched to Burnt Hickory, and on the 25th to New Hope Church, some four miles north of Dallas. Here Geary's (Second) Division, marching on the left of Williams', struck the enemy in force. The First Division at once marched back to his support, and here again the stuff of which the American volunteer is made was evident. When Hooker decided to drive the enemy from his position here he accompanied Robinson's Brigade, of which the Sixty-first and Eighty-second regiments formed part, in the advance, and on witnessing the steadiness of the men during a difficult movement performed with the utmost precision under a galling fire he turned to General Robinson and said, "That was splendidly done, General!" Quite a number were killed and wounded here, among the latter being Comrade Mullen. Having driven the enemy from his positions here after very severe fighting, the First Division remained in the vicinity of Dallas until June 1, 1864, although in the meantime, on the 28th to 31st, Robinson's brigade guarded a supply train for ammunition to Kingston, Georgia, and return.

The first part of June, 1864, was occupied by maneuvers in the vicinity of Kennesaw Mountain, with many changes of position and some fighting, attended by a number of casualties. On the 5th the brigade was near Pine Knob, and on the 6th moved to the left of Burnt Hickory, near Mt. Olive Church. After some minor movements it took up position a few miles south and remained there 11th to 15th. On June 16th, in a skirmish some men were wounded. On the 17th, the Regiment moved further south, still skirmishing, some casualties resulting. On the 19th and 20th it formed part of the force attacking Kennesaw Mountain, losing some men. Then, resuming the southward movement it went into position before a strong line of the enemy's works at Kolb's (or Culp's) farm, a few miles west of Marietta, Georgia, on June 22, 1864. Here, while Robinson's Brigade was taking position, it was fiercely attacked by the enemy, who was handsomely repulsed. In this affair the Sixty-first, led by the gallant McGroarty, pursued the enemy to his works, and after running great risk of annihilation, or capture, returned safely to its position, bringing in a number of prisoners, including three armed men, whom Comrade Harris captured unaided, by the ruse of commanding an imaginary squad in the darkness. It was here that the lamented Major Beckett lost his life while charging the enemy. The command lay here for several days, in the meantime strengthening its position by constructing rifle pits.

On July 1, 1864, the command moved out, and on the 6th reached the Chattahoochie river, to find that the Confederate troops had evacuated their strong works there. On the 17th the column crossed the river at Pace's Ferry, and took up positions on the south side. On the 18th marched to near Buckhead and on the 19th to Peachtree Creek.

Here on July 20, 1864, the Sixty-first and Eighty-second regiments took a conspicuous part in one of the bloodiest battles of the war, considering the numbers engaged. The enemy, coming out from his works, attempted to take advantage of the Federal columns while they were crossing the stream, and before all were over attacked the Third Division (Butterfield's), which formed the left. Gaining some temporary advantage here he then attacked the First Division (Williams'), of which Robinson's Third Brigade formed a part, and here occurred some of the most desperate fighting of the campaign. Rapidly forming under fire, the division received the enemy's charge, made with an impetuosity that brought him right into the Federal lines, and resulted in much hand to hand fighting, of which Robinson's Brigade did its full share. After a bitter struggle victory rested with the Union troops, and the Confederates were driven from the field. It was here that Colonel McGroarty lost an arm and Lieutenant Colonel Bown a leg. The latter died a few weeks later in the hospital in Chattanooga, Tennessee, and McGroarty's wound was the leading cause of his death in Cincinnati, Ohio, a few years later [1870], although he continued in the service until the close of the war. Lieutenant Colonel Thompson of the Eighty-second Ohio was also wounded here, and both regiments lost very heavily in killed, wounded and missing, the number in the Sixty-first being 74 out of 174 in action.

In front of the regiment's position were counted 78 dead Confederates and 188 of their rifles were picked up there. In the final charge the Sixty-first Ohio captured the colors of the Sixty-first South Carolina, and took as prisoners its Colonel, two Captains, three Lieutenants, the color bearer and 29 privates.

The next day, July 21, 1864, Captain E. H. Newcomb met his death under peculiarly tragic circumstances. Reconnoitering to the front, entirely unattended, he ran into a small outpost of the enemy. Disdaining their command to surrender, he charged on them with only his saber for a weapon, and reluctantly they were obliged to shoot him down. They gave his body an honorable burial on the spot, and erected a large headboard, on which the particulars of the affair were carved. The inscription ended with, "He was the bravest Yankee we ever saw."

After the Battle of Peachtree Creek the troops moved to the front to Atlanta and remained there until July 27th, when the Twentieth Corps was ordered back to guard the fords of the Chattahoochie. Here it remained until August 5th, when it returned to the vicinity of Atlanta, and took position in the lines of investment and participated in the siege.

Even before Atlanta was evacuated General Sherman was preparing another advance, and after equipping his army anew, on November 15, 1864, the "March of the Sea" began. On this campaign the Sixty-first, all of its field officers dead or wounded, was commanded by Captain John Garrett, the senior officer present for duty. This campaign to Savannah, while not accompanied by the exciting events of battles fought and victories won, was a glorious one in its results. Although there was very little fighting on this march there was work to do in the way of destroying railroad tracks, building corduroy roads and constructing bridges. And so by easy marches, subsisting off the country, in part, the great army advanced toward the Atlantic coast.

On the night of November 15, 1864, the command camped east of Decatur, Georgia, and on the 20th at Eatonton. On the 21st the march was resumed toward Milledgeville, and on the 22nd and 23rd were in the vicinity of that town. Here, in the old Capitol, General Robinson went through the form of reorganizing the state government, and for one day at least Georgia was loyal to the Union, through the repealing of the ordinance of secession. Here also many a poor soldier became a millionaire for the time being through the possession of unlimited quantities of Confederate notes and bonds found in the vaults.

Crossing the Oconee here the troops camped several miles out from Milledgeville on November 24th. On the night of the 25th it was a few miles west of Sandersonville, and on the 26th, passing through that hamlet, the command stopped a few miles south. On the 27th it was at Davisboro, and on the night of the 28th the Corps camped on the west bank of the Ogeechee, near Louisville, Georgia, the First Division taking position at Speers Station, a few miles south.

On December 1st the bivouac was a few miles east of the Ogeechee, and on December 2nd at Buckhead. The halt on December 3rd was at Horse Creek, and December 4th and 5th a few miles south of Sylvania. On the 6th the march was continued and on December 7th Springfield, between the Ogeechee and Savannah Rivers was reached. The movement continued on the 8th, and on the 9th the affair on Montieth Swamp took place. The enemy had a small earthwork here, which he vacated hastily after some ineffective firing, as the charging Sixty-first and Eighty-second reached it. A few prisoners were taken here.

On December 10, 1864, Sherman's troops settled down in front of the Confederate defenses of Savannah, and the "March to the Sea" ended—a march conducted with strict regard for the rules of civilized warfare, with the greatest consideration for non-combatants, and with a self-restraint under great provocation never surpassed in any campaign.

No property was taken for subsistence of the army that was not paid for then or later, no inhabited houses were plundered or burned,

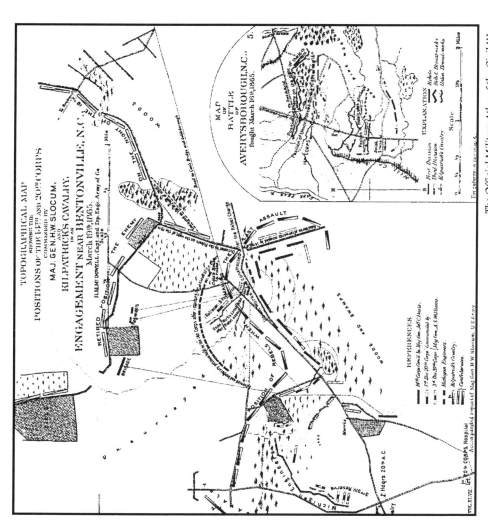

The Official Military Atlas of the Civil War

and no self-respecting woman has cause to complain of the conduct of the soldiers. Cotton, the source of all the wealth of the Confederate government, was contraband-of-war and was destroyed wherever found, and necessarily the buildings containing it. Aside from this there was no destruction by the organized troops. Some marauding by lately freed slaves and irresponsible camp-followers there was; but there could be no very great destruction in a sparsely settled country almost destitute of wealth, either material or portable. So much for the still harped on "outrages of Sherman's men."

With some changes of position the troops lay in front of Savannah until the capitulation of the place, December 21, 1864. Soon afterwards Robinson's brigade was stationed at the McAlpine Place, four miles from the city, on the river bank, and the Sixty-first was detached for duty in the city.

About the middle of January, 1865, the movement of Sherman's army through South Carolina began. On January 17th most of the Twentieth Corps crossed the Savannah River and marched through the rice swamps to Purysburg, South Carolina, reaching there January 19th. On account of high water it was impossible to move further until the 27th, when the march was resumed and the vicinity of Robertsville was reached. Here the Sixty-first having come up from Savannah with a portion of Geary's division, joined its brigade.

On account of the flooded condition of the country further movement was suspended until February 4, 1865, when the march was resumed. From here on for some time the campaign northward was a series of daily uneventful marches, with much building of corduroy roads to enable the trains and artillery to pass through the swampy country. On February 8th the command crossed the north fork of the Edisto and camped a few miles north of that river. On the 15th and 16th the column was in the vicinity of Columbia, South Carolina, and from a distance witnessed the destruction of that city, which was fired by the evacuating Confederates in destroying the immense amount of cotton belonging to the Confederacy stored in the numerous warehouses.

On February 17th the regiment camped on the south bank of the Saluda River, and on the 19th on the south bank of the Broad. On the 20th, they passed Winnsboro and reached the Catawba (or Wateree) River on the 21st, crossing that stream on the 23rd near Rocky Mount Post Office. The Sixty-first was at Chesterfield on March 2nd and by the 3rd was on the Great Peede, about the 6th, and reached Fayetteville, North Carolina March 11, 1865. On the 14th, 15th and 16th the regiment advanced up the east side of the Cape Fear River, and on the morning of the 16th found the enemy in position some three miles south of Averysboro, North Carolina. After stubborn resistance his advanced lines were forced back to his works, and after nightfall he withdrew. In this affair the Sixty-first and Eighty-second suffered some loss.

On March 18th the troops resumed the march, crossing the Black River and advancing toward Goldsboro, North Carolina. On the morning of the 19th sounds of a severe engagement were heard on the left. The column was at once dispatched in that direction, and it was found that the Fourteenth Corps was heavily engaged near Bentonville, North Carolina. Robinson's brigade was thrown in to fill a gap in the line and was soon hotly engaged. The troops on the left giving way, the brigade was forced back by an overwhelming force on its flank, as well as in its front. Hardly had a new line been formed a short distance in the rear, with the artillery now in a position to render aid, than the enemy assaulted again, more furiously, if possible, than before. This time he was repulsed, as he was in several charges made later. Finding it impossible to break the Federal lines, the enemy withdrew in the night and in this, the last battle in which Robinson's brigade was engaged, the Union arms were victorious.

On the next day the enemy retired before the advance of the Federal troops, and after this defeat the disintegration of the Confederate forces, which had already begun was rapid.

The march to Goldsboro, North Carolina, was now resumed and that place was reached March 24, 1865. It was here, on April 9, 1865, in pursuance of War Department orders of March 31st, that what remained of the Sixty-first and Eighty-second Regiments were consolidated and the new regiment numbered the Eighty-second. Colonel McGroarty, who had now returned minus the arm left at Peachtree Creek, Georgia, was in command, and on May 1, 1865 was brevetted Brigadier General.

On April 10, 1865, the troops marched to Raleigh, North Carolina, and on the 30th began the march to Washington, via Richmond, reaching Alexandria, Virginia, May 19th. On the 24th it participated in the Grand Review by President Johnson, and all the great notables of the government in Washington, Sherman's troops exciting most favorable comment by their soldiers bearing and excellent marching.

Soon afterwards the grand old Twentieth Corps was dissolved, and the Eighty-second became part of a provisional division of the Fourteenth Corps. On June 5, 1865, the regiment was sent to Louisville, Kentucky, and was there mustered out of the United States service on July 24, 1865.

Its marches and campaigns had been in or through the states of West Virginia, Virginia, Maryland, Pennsylvania, Ohio, Indiana, Kentucky, Tennessee, Alabama, Georgia, South Carolina, North Carolina and the District of Columbia. Many of its members found graves on a score of battlefields; others died in hospitals from their wounds, and

Col. Stephen J. McGroarty and staff
Mass. MOLLUS Collection, USAMHI

many more from disease, while a few pined their lives away in Southern prisons. Of the thousand untrained men who, in April 1862, filled with enthusiasm, had marched form Camp Chase, but a fragment returned—the peers of any soldier in the world in discipline, in courage and in efficiency.

So ends the story of the Sixty-first Ohio Volunteers. Its campaigns and battles form a part of the history of the nation. The names of its dead are inscribed on the imperishable roll of honor. No blush of shame is called to the cheek of its surviving members at thought of any incident in its career. That it did not achieve a famously brilliant record was not the fault of its Colonel, the lamented McGroarty, nor of its devoted followers. It was simply because opportunity did not offer. As it was, the regiment did its duty as it came to it, sometimes faring well, sometimes faring ill; today exultant in victory, tomorrow despondent in defeat, but its members never losing faith in the ultimate result.

Partial List of Losses

Abbott, Barnett, killed, Freeman's Ford, Va.
Albright, John W., wounded, Gettysburg, Pa.
Arbuckle, Lieut. John, wounded, Freeman's Ford, Va.
Baker, Clement, captured, Culpepper C.H., Va., Died in Prison
Bales, Herman, killed, Peachtree Creek, Ga.
Barrett, Enos, captured, Chancellorsville, Va.
Beaver, James, wounded, Peachtree Creek, Ga.
Beckett, Major David C., killed, Kolb's Farm, Ga.
Bevard, Henry, wounded and captured, Gettysburg, Pa.
Bevard, Joseph, captured. Died in prison.
Biddle, Abrose, mortally wounded, Peachtree Creek, Ga.
Bown, Lieut. Col. William H.H., mortally wounded, Peachtree Creek, Ga.
Brent, Lieut. Edmund V., wounded, Gettysburg, Pa.
Brewer, Paris A., wounded, Peachtree Creek, Ga.
Buckler, Conrad, killed, Peachtree Creek, Ga.
Callahan, Alex., killed, Dallas, Ga.
Cavanaugh, John, wounded, Peachtree Creek, Ga.
Christy, Samuel, wounded, Peachtree Creek, Ga.
Collins, John, wounded, Chancellorsville, Va.
Daly, Thomas, killed, Dallas, Ga.
Deardorf, Edgar, mortally wounded, Chancellorsville, Va.
Devany, Patrick, wounded, Gettysburg, Pa.
Dunn, James, wounded, Chancellorsville, Va.
Ecord, James C., wounded, Chancellorsville, Va.
Fleharty, Perry A., captured, Chancellorsville, Va.
Fleharty, Perry A., wounded, Dallas, Ga.
Fults, George W., mortally wounded, Freeman's Ford, Va.

Frank, Joel, killed, Peachtree Creek, Ga.
Gilleran, Thomas, killed, Gettysburg, Pa.
Ginley, Jeremiah, killed, Peachtree Creek, Ga.
Grace, Jeremiah J., wounded, Freeman's Ford, Va.
Grafton, James W., killed, Peachtree Creek, Ga.
Guillaume, John, wounded, Gettysburg, Pa.
Hamling, Henry, captured, Gettysburg, Pa.
Hammond, David F., killed, Resacca, Ga.
Harris, George W., captured, Gettysburg, Pa.
Heck, Michael, wounded, Chancellorsville, Va.
Henny, Peter, captured, Smithville, N.C.
Hehl, Michael, killed, Dallas, Ga.
Holly, Wm. H., captured, March 17, 1865.
Horn, Patrick, killed, Peachtree Creek, Ga.
Idel, Josiah, captured, Chancellorsville, Va.
Jones, John, killed, Peachtree Creek, Ga.
Justus, William E., killed, Peachtree Creek, Ga.
Kirtz, George W., mortally wounded, Peachtree Creek, Ga.
Larkin, George, wounded, Gettysburg, Pa.
Leifer, Jacob, captured, Gettysburg, Pa.
Leifer, Marcus T., killed, Peachtree Creek, Ga.
Lenihan, John, wounded, Gettysburg, Pa.
Long, David B., wounded, Peachtree Creek, Ga.
Lydon, William, captured, Chancellorsville, Va.
McCauley, John, wounded, Freeman's Ford, Va.
McCluskey, Michael, killed, Atlanta, Ga.
McDonald, Dennis, killed, Peachtree Creek, Ga.
McGroarty, Colonel Stephen J., wounded, Peachtree Creek, Ga.
McGroarty, Captain William H., killed, Lookout Valley, Tenn.
McShane, Edw., wounded, Peachtree Creek, Ga.
Mackey, James, killed, Kolb's Farm, Ga.
Mangan, John, wounded ———
Masterson, Thomas, wounded, Gettysburg, Pa.
Mattlinger, Lieut. Samuel, wounded, Chancellorsville, Va
May, George W., captured, Gettysburg, Pa.
Michael, Jacob, killed, Kennesaw Mountain, Ga.
Moon, Thomas, wounded ———
Moore, Asst. Surg. Wm. B., killed, Gettysburg, Pa.
Morgan, William H., wounded, Freeman's Ford, Va.
Mullen, Theo., wounded, Dallas, Ga.
Murty, John C., captured, Chancellorsville, Va.
Newcomb, Captain Edw. H., killed, Atlanta, Ga.
Obenour, Ephraim, wounded and captured, Gettysburg, Pa.
Oyer, Jonas, wounded ———
Pence, Samuel, wounded, Chancellorsville, Va.

Rallston, Alfred H., killed, Freeman's Ford, Va.
Rank, John, killed, Freeman's Ford, Va.
Ranney, Edw. G., killed, Gettysburg, Pa.
Reynolds, Captain James M., killed, Gettysburg, Pa.
Reese, Henry, killed, Peachtree Creek, Ga.
Richards, James D., killed, Peachtree Creek, Ga.
Rosenburg, Gustavus, captured, Culpepper C.H., Va.
Ross, John, died Aug. 8, 1864, of wounds received in action.
Rupert, John, captured, Chancellorsville, Va.
Schurar, Jacob, missing, Bentonville, N.C.
Sherman, B.F., killed, Gettysburg, Pa.
Sibzell, B.F., wounded, Freeman's Ford, Va.
Smallwood, Isaac W., wounded, Chancellorsville, Va.
Smith, Thomas, wounded, Dallas, Ga.
Spellman, Cornelius, killed, Peachtree Creek, Ga.
Starrott, John L., killed, Second Bull Run, Va.
Stephens, Alexander, killed, Freeman's Ford, Va.
Strauer, Andrew, mortally wounded, Peachtree Creek, Va.
Sullivan, Lieut. Daniel O., wounded, Gettysburg, Pa.
Taylor, William, captured ———
Thompson, Alfred G., missing, Atlanta, Ga.
Travers, Martin, killed, Freeman's Ford, Va.
Turbyville, John, killed, Gettysburg, Pa.
Wallace, Captain Frederick S., wounded, Gettysburg, Pa.
Walters, Strod, mortally wounded, Second Bull Run, Va.
Warner, William, killed, Kennesaw Mountain, Ga.
Waucher, Charles, wounded, Freeman's Ford, Va.
Wheatly, John, mortally wounded, Chancellorsville, Va.
Whitesel, John, wounded, Second Bull Run, Va.
Williams, Aristarchus H., killed, Gettysburg, Pa.
Williams, Lieut. Daniel W., killed, Gettysburg, Pa.
Zebold, Samuel E., killed, Peachtree Creek, Ga.

Incomplete records show that seventy-one died of disease in hospitals.

Capt. Henry R. Bending, Company I, 61st Ohio Volunteer Infantry
Roger D. Hunt Collection, USAMHI

The Battle of Chancellorsville

By James H. Peabody
Formerly First Sergeant, Company "B"
Sixty-first Ohio Volunteer Infantry

(First published in G.A.R. War Papers, Fred C. Jones Post, No. 401, Department of Ohio, G.A.R.)

In relating my recollections of the Battle of Chancellorsville, I trust you will excuse my use of the first person. Being one of the number mixed up in the mess, it can not very well be avoided.

We left our camp at Acquia Creek, and marched twenty-five or thirty miles up the Rappahannock River, crossing it at Germania Ford on pontoons, at night, and camped four or five miles farther on about midnight, no one being allowed to build fires that night. I do not remember exactly how many days elapsed from the time we left Acquia Creek until we arrived at or near Dowdall's Tavern, about three miles beyond the Chancellorsville House. It was on the 1st of May, I think, in the afternoon, that we arrived, and about four or five o'clock each division was drawn up, column doubled on the center, closed *en masse*, to listen to an order from General Hooker, congratulating the army on its successful movement in flanking Lee out of his position at Fredericksburg.

The next morning, May 2, we were up early, left camp, and moved along the road until we came to the place which we occupied at the time Jackson made his "dash." We then took our position along this road which skirted a woods, there being an open field in the front, I think not more than two or three hundred yards wide; then, as we supposed, an open woods, but which, however, proved to be a swamp. Our pickets were thrown out to the edge of the woods, we stacked arms in the road, and broke ranks with strict orders to be ready to "fall in" at an instant's warning. The boys spread themselves out in the woods, threw off their knapsacks, and it was not long before they had all the rest of their traps off, and many of them playing "draw poker." The Sixty-first Ohio Volunteer Infantry, to which I belonged, was in the First Brigade, Third

Division, commanded by General Schurz. The First Division, under command of General Devens, was on our right; the Second Division, under General Steinwehr, on our left; and the Corps on the extreme right of Hooker's line. During the forenoon some of our pickets came in, said they were on the edge of a swamp and had tried to see how far out they could get in it, but found they could go only a short distance, and did not believe any one could get through it. They also reported that they could see a line of flankers in front of them, moving toward our right, and a line of dust beyond. We remained there idle nearly all day, while the enemy kept moving in front of us to our right. I will here insert an order of General Hooker which was issued at half-past nine in the morning— General Jackson not making his charge until nearly or quite six in the evening—and will also state General Hooker sent Graham's Brigade and a battery from General Sickles' Corps to strengthen our right, but General Howard refused to accept it.

Headquarters Army of the Potomac
Chancellorsville, May 2, 1863, 9:30 A.M.

Major-Generals Howard and Slocum:

I am directed by the Major-General commanding to say that the disposition you have made of your corps has been with the view to a front attack by the enemy. If he should throw himself upon your flank, he wishes you to examine the ground and determine upon the position you will take in that event, in order that you may be prepared for him in whatever direction he advances. He suggests that you have heavy reserves well in hand to meet this contingency. The right of your line does not appear to be strong enough. No artificial defenses worth naming have been thrown up, and there appears to be a scarcity of troops at that point, and not, in the General's opinion, as favorably posted as might be. We have good reasons to suppose that the enemy is moving to our right. Please advance your pickets for purposed of observation as far as may be safe, in order to obtain timely information of their approach.

(Signed) J.H. Van Alen
Brigadier General and Aide-de-Camp

The situation was about the same in the other divisions as it was in ours. Colonel Lee, of the Fifty-fifth Ohio was officer of the day and had charge of their picket line. When his pickets reported to him what the enemy were doing, he informed Brigadier General Nathaniel C. McLean, who was in command of that brigade. Together with other officers, they went to the skirmish line and saw for themselves what was going on, and then sent word to General Devens, who in turn sent word to General Howard, suggesting the propriety of changing the front. No notice was taken of it, and, after an hour or so, they again dispatched word to General Howard, that the enemy were massing on our right, this time asking if they might change front; still no attention was paid to them. General Devens placed two regiments facing the right; General Schurz, who was also uneasy about the situation, placed in the rear of his division a small brigade in close double column facing the right. General Steinwehr already had, by Howard's order, Barlow's brigade of about twenty-five hundred men in his rear; but General Howard allowed, without protest, this brigade to be taken away and sent to re-enforce General Sickles. After waiting in vain for the desired permission, they again, for the third time, notified General Howard that the enemy were massing in force on our right flank, and begging that they might change front so our right would rest on the river. He then condescended to send back this order: "No. Hold the position you now have; you are more scared than hurt." In less than half an hour from the time he sent that reply, Jackson, with his whole corps of twenty-two thousand men, and with all the impetuosity he possessed, charged the right flank and rear of the Eleventh Corps. At this time our arms were stacked in the road, the boys still playing "draw poker"; but when they heard the whistle of bullets, concluded not to play longer.

That was the situation our brigade was in when the bullets began whistling over our heads along the flank. No one ever saw men hustle on their traps and get into line any quicker than we did; each man picked up everything he had, not one of them leaving anything behind; and by the time we had gotten into line and taken arms, they had crowded us so much from the right as to turn me "right about." As I looked up along the line, I saw a piece of shell, or chunk of iron, coming with a ricochet along down the side hill—it was from the first gun fired—and the first thing I knew it struck me on the ankle, knocking my foot out from under me. My first thought was that I had lost my heel, but, glancing down, couldn't see anything missing. By this time, the right had been driven back pell-mell; in fact, the whole line was broken. It would not have been good generalship on my part to have stopped and made a close examination, so I followed the rest. As we emerged from the woods into an open field, I saw a sight I shall never forget as long as I live. There were regiments, brigades and divisions completely disorganized and scattered; in the midst was General Howard and staff, or part of it; on the extreme right of that scattered line was a small body of men—which I afterward learned was McLean's Brigade of the First Division—making a desperate attempt to check the advance of the enemy. I saw General Howard swinging his revolver in his left hand—he had no right hand—and when I had gotten close to him, he was crying out, "Halt! Halt! I'm ruined, I'm ruined; I'll shoot if you don't stop; I'm ruined, I'm ruined," over and over again. I stopped, leaned on my musket, and looked at him in surprise and wonder, that a man who occupied the position he did should get so completely confused and bewildered; in fact, he was "rattled."

While I was standing there admiring the self-possession of the General, there was a Reb got among us some way, no one knew how; he did not have any gun, only a knapsack, haversack and canteen. Some of the boys asked him how he got there, where he came from, and many other questions, but he wouldn't give any account of himself, and edged off; finally started to run toward our rear bearing to our left. He paid no attention to repeated calls to halt, and had not run more than one hundred or fifty feet or so, before two or three of our men threw up their guns and shot him dead; he fell headlong on his face and lay there.

After the Reb was disposed of, I again looked over to our right and could see, coming out of the woods, a line, or rather mass, of Rebs, still on the flank of McLean's Brigade, which compelled them to give way. There was no use fighting against such odds. I then turned again to General Howard, who was looking in the same direction, and when he comprehended the situation, he put "spurs" to his horse and rode to the rear of our right, or in that direction. I thought he was going there to impart the same information to them he had given us; that is, "I'm ruined." None of us knew or cared where he went. Then there was another break for the rear pell-mell, which was kept up until the enemy was finally checked by massing the artillery near the Chancellorsville House. After order had been brought out of chaos, and the regiments and brigades found their proper places, we camped in rear of the Chancellorsville House. Then it was that I found time to pull off my shoe and stocking to examine my ankle, and found a small flesh wound about the size of a silver quarter; it having been a glancing blow, didn't do much damage, only made a sore.

The next morning we moved back toward the United States Ford, formed a line along the road facing a wooded ravine, and there built small breastworks. Nothing of importance occurred here, except that one night, while all were asleep, some two or three on the skirmish line fired. That started the whole line, all raised up in a second; and, after waiting until the pickets came in, fired. One fellow lying near me, I think it was Jim Yeazel, raised up on his haunches, elevated his gun at an angle of about forty-five degrees, blazed away, laid his gun down, then laid down himself and went to sleep again. There was only one round fired. The next day there was a dead cow found in front of the skirmish line. We remained here until the 5th or 6th, when the army recrossed the river at the United States Ford, and we got back to our old camp at Acquia Creek on the 6th or 7th, after marching through thin, slushy mud from four to fourteen inches deep.

Before passing judgment, let us look at the situation: Here is the Eleventh Corps, with only ten thousand men, drawn up in line along the road skirting a woods; a short distance in front is an impenetrable swamp; in front of that is a road parallel to and about one mile from the one we occupied; about a mile or so in our rear runs a river; the country is undulating, partially densely wooded, partially open fields and some swamps; we lying there guarding the swamp nearly all day, not lifting a finger toward making fortifications or defenses of any kind, giving General Jackson plenty of time to march his corps of twenty-two thousand men along that road in front of us to our right flank, General Howard being repeatedly notified, not only by officers and men of his own corps, but from Sickles' Corps and Pleasanton's cavalry, and not only refusing to heed the warning, but insulting them by telling them that their stories were only the offspring of their diseased imaginations, or their fears.

I will admit that Jackson ought to have had brains enough to charge Howard's front through the swamp; but no, he was ignorant and ill-mannered enough to creep around to the right flank and rear. But Howard had his position in front of that swamp, one in which he could defy Lee's whole army; he was going to hold that position, and the idea that those colonels should send to him, advising a change of front, so that his right would be protected by the river, and his left by the swamp, or that he would need any fortifications, was too absurd. Of course, he would not change his line of battle. What did those fellows on the skirmish line know about it? They were only colonels. He was a major-general. So Jackson had plenty of time in which to place his men just as he wanted, by forming Rodes' Division on one side of the road, in which our line was formed; Colston's Division on the other side, only two hundred yards apart; with Hill's Division and Fitzhugh Lee's Brigade of cavalry on the road and just in their rear, the whole line perpendicular, too, and overlapping ours, both front and rear, and when he got good and ready, made his charge. The result was, he doubled up Howard's right, and again doubled and redoubled the Eleventh Corps of only ten thousand to his twenty-two thousand men; but, instead of taking any steps toward checking Jackson's continual flank movements, Howard must needs rush among his own men, swing his revolver and whine: "I'm ruined." No, the Eleventh Corps did not ruin General Howard; but he ruined the reputation of the Eleventh Corps forever.

The burning shame of that stigma has followed us for nearly twenty-eight years, and will follow us on to the grave, and still on to the end of time. Many times I have hesitated to admit having been in the Eleventh Corps. I am perfectly willing to acknowledge, if you were to form a line of battle with a corps of mules, it would be right and proper to place them with their tails to the front, as that would be the position in which they could most successfully resist the charge of an enemy. But if you form a line of battle of soldiers in that same manner, you must expect them to use their heels also, and you'll not be disappointed.

There was not a corps in all the army during the entire war, from the first battle of Bull Run, July 21, 1861, until Appamattox, April 8-9, 1865, that was ever drawn up in line to resist the charge of an enemy in such inexcusable stupidity as General Howard formed the Eleventh Corps at Chancellorsville; and had they not run, General Lee would have the entire corps with which to place additional ornaments inside Libby, Belle Isle and Andersonville, with the Major-General as the chief ornament.

I will say this for General Howard: There was not a man in the corps that ever for one moment questioned his courage or loyalty, for there was not a more brave or loyal man in all the army than he; but no man in that corps had any confidence in his judgment at critical times after Chancellorsville. I have given you the best description I could of only that part of the fight that I saw myself.

On May 2, at Dowdall's Tavern, Jackson, with twenty-two thousand men, routed Howard with ten thousand. May 3, at Fairview, Stuart with thirty-seven thousand men, defeated Sickles and Couch with thirty-two thousand. The same day at Salem Church, four Confederate brigades of ten thousand men defeated Brooks with nine thousand. May 4 at Banks' Ford, Lee with twenty-five thousand men defeated Sedgewick, with twenty thousand. So you see, Lee, with his superior skill and knowledge of the country, brought more men in at the fighting points than Hooker, although Hooker actually had much the largest army. But Howard was the only general to allow the enemy to come in on both flank and rear with more than double numbers. You all know that whenever there was a decided victory won, how ready the commanding general was to receive the credit and honor of winning that victory. I have noticed when any portion of the army met with a disastrous defeat, the commanding general was just as ready and willing to accord the enlisted men the credit and honor of winning that defeat. I make no apology for the Eleventh Corps, but no man, who knows nothing whatever about the circumstances attending that engagement has any right to make sweeping and unjust criticisms. I personally know there were men in that corps who were just as brave as any who ever trod a battlefield. There never has been an army that was suddenly and violently struck square on an unprotected flank, that has been able to resist that blow; it can do only one of two things—stand and be shot in the back, powerless to make any defense, or run. I had no desire to ornament the inside of any Rebel prison-pen, and didn't want to sit down on a bullet hole either.

From Stafford Heights to Gettysburg in 1863

By Leonidas M. Jewett
Late Captain, Sixty-first Ohio Volunteer Infantry
Brevet Major, U.S.V.

(First published in Sketches of War History, 1861–1865,
of the Commandery of the State of Ohio Military Order of the Loyal Legion
of the United States, Vol. V, Pages 213–222)

Thirty-nine years have passed since we broke camp at Stafford Heights to begin what turned out to be the greatest and most eventful march of my experience. The memories of Chancellorsville, like dark shadows, still linger in the minds of the boys that participated in that great disaster. Never had hopes been so high, and failure so great.

On April 27, 1863, we marched from Stafford Court House to Hartwood Church. Those of us of the rank and file had not forgotten the identical march between exactly the same places two months before, and wondered where we were going. Frankly, with the scenes of Chancellorsville and the tangled forest then so fresh in our memories, we had no desire to re-experience another visit across the river. There was one precious reflection that, whatever we were destined to go to, the Stone Wall would not again ride around our flank in open defiance, and again destroy our boys. The march from Hartwood Church to Catlett's Station, crossing Manassas Junction to Centerville on June 14th, dispelled all illusions as to our again having to cross the Rappahannock. How the oppressive heat, fatigue and toil of the march of that day linger in the memory of the writer and his old comrades who joined in the procession! The three days spent at Centerville brought up old memories of the August days of the year before at Bull Run and the surrounding country for many a mile. Old Throughfare Gap, in the magnificent range of the Blue Mountains, and the plains of Manassas are a sight to make you smile as a lover of nature, and to make you cry as a soldier. That moonlight scene of the boys in blue going into position at Bull Run on the night before the commencement of the battle was to me the grandest and most impressive scene of the war. Miles of lines of Union blue, with muskets gleaming in the moonlight, lying down for rest, preparatory for the great battle of the next day, made me think, boy that I was, that the war would soon come to an end. Little did I know of the great masses of soldiers in gray on the other side that were at the same time taking position to fight the battle of the next day, and less did I know of the failure of two or three Union corps within the sound of our guns to come to our relief as we fought the battle of the 29th and 30th of August of 1862, and after more than thirty years of careful study I know less now than then. It was a battle of great endurance, unrivaled gallantry and desperate fighting, but, alas, we came back to Centerville in the early dawn of that Sunday morning in the mist and rain, a defeated army. Pardon this digression, for I am marching with the army in 1863, and had gotten as far along as Centerville, and I could not avoid referring to some of the thoughts that will linger in my memory as long as I shall be permitted to breathe the pure air of the great country we helped to save.

June 17, 1863, we left Centerville, passing Gum Springs and Leesburg, and camped on Goose Creek, remaining there until the 24th. The frequent reconnaissances of infantry, the scouting cavalry, and the distant cannonading beyond the Blue Ridge, suggested that we were near the center, and our enemies upon the other side, upon the circumference of the circle. The Goose Creek days were anxious ones, and we felt that the battle would soon come on; but where or under what circumstances was the problem yet unsolved. June 24th broke the monotony, for on that day we marched to the Potomac River at Edward's Ferry and camped for the night. It began to dawn upon us that the battle was to be fought somewhere upon the free soil of the loyal States of the North. How much that meant, then, how little is known about it now except by my old comrades! It was an exciting and eventful period of the war, as we on the morning of the 25th crossed the Potomac River into the beautiful Monocacy Valley of Maryland, and in the heat of that summer day, marched twenty-six miles to Jeffersonville. What a contrast with the barren worn-out lands of old Virginia, with its pine-clad hills and mountains, and everlasting oceans of evergreen to the rich and fertile fields of Maryland and Pennsylvania! How the fresh milk, bread and butter, and everything good to eat, were enjoyed by the boys. It was to us a land of milk and honey, to say nothing of many other good things to drink that went into the old canteen as we marched along. As we remained in the next few days near Middletown, we had a glimpse of the South Mountain battlefield, where McClellan and his troops had, the year before, won victory for our flag, the spot where the gallant Major General Reno fell being pointed out to us. The inspiration of this historic battlefield is to me one of the precious memories of this eventful march from Stafford Heights to Gettysburg.

The occurrences of the 28th of June were, in my judgment, the turning point of this famous campaign, and more important to the Union cause than even the repulse of Pickett's charge at Gettysburg.

I will, in some detail, endeavor to elaborate what I consider the only thought attempted to be expressed in this paper, aided by the most careful reflection of many years. We spent the forenoon of the 28th at Middletown, and witnessed the march of the Third Corps, under the gallant Sickles and Birney, and never did I observe a more inspiring sight, and a finer body of men never marched than the veterans of this historic corps, full of life, as light-hearted and gay as the birds that flew across the valley to the beautiful mountains that surrounded us on every hand. In the afternoon we marched to Frederick City. It must be admitted upon all sides that the strategical movements of Hooker up to this time had been all that military science could exact. But it is right here that a danger confronted the Federal army as great as when Hooker stopped in the wilderness at Chancellorsville and failed to march ahead and uncover Banks' Ford, and get into communication with the troops he had left under Sedgwick at Fredericksburg. Hooker wanted the troops at Harper's Ferry, under French, to be placed under his immediate command, as it was, no doubt, his idea to add to this command the Twelfth Corps of General Slocum, and go up the Cumberland Valley in the rear of the Confederate army, while the rest of Hooker's army should march on the line that Meade took to Gettysburg. This plan would have placed the Catoctin and other ranges of mountains between the two wings of Hooker's army, with no chance of uniting them until the near vicinity of Gettysburg was reached, and this union would be practically impossible by reason of the presence of Lee's army. Bearing in mind that Lee was in communication with his whole army of infantry, and able to mass it rapidly upon a given point, we would have been whipped in detail by a hopeless inability to concentrate our whole army. The same mistake would have occurred that Napoleon made in detaching Grouchy from his main army at Waterloo. There Napoleon did not know where Blucher had gone after Ligny, while Hooker knew, or ought to have known, that Lee was able in a short time to concentrate his whole army upon a given point. It is not my purpose to criticize a General under whose command I had the honor to serve in the Army of the Potomac, and in the great campaign from Chattanooga to Atlanta in 1864, and whose memory is cherished by me as one of the most illustrious soldiers of the war.

Several things happened to defeat the threatened disaster that might have befallen us by reason of the proposed division of our army while on the Gettysburg march:

(1) The refusal of General Halleck to place the troops of General French at Harper's Ferry under the command of General Hooker.

(2) The resignation of General Hooker of the command of the Army of the Potomac, and its acceptance by the President.

(3) The placing of General Meade in command on the night of the 28th. Meade had skillfully aided in the May before at Chancellorsville in the night retreat, and the dangers and perils of a divided army were too fresh in his mind to again attempt to divide his troops by ranges of mountains, rendering communication impossible, and while he possessed the confidence of the government in the highest degree, he was given the unlimited command of General French's troops. Be it remembered as a monument to his military skill that he never thought of any movement that did not contemplate the concentration, with reasonable dispatch, of his whole army upon a given point. His ability and true eye as a military engineer, taught him the old maxim, "there is safety in union."

The government did not have confidence in General Hooker's ability to manage a large army after the affair at Chancellorsville. His magnificent strategy in warding off Lee and watching his every movement in our march up to June 28th, gave no excuse for his removal, but his unwise plan to divide his army and to get authority to control French for that purpose, did not meet the approval of the authorities at Washington, and his resignation was the opportunity long sought by the wiley Halleck and the illustrious Secretary of War Stanton, for his removal from the command, as evidenced by the prompt sending of Colonel Hardie to the midnight camp, placing Meade in command, and taking Hooker with him to Baltimore. It seems to me at this late day that these occurrences were as important to the Union cause as the great battle of a few days afterwards. It makes us think that there was a great Providence directing our destiny in the direction of Union success. It was a critical time in the history of the war. A disaster upon the soil of the great free North would, we fear, have invited foreign recognition of the Confederate States, and, to say the least, a serious prolongation of the great struggle. June 29th we marched to Emmittsburg, and remained there during the 30th. The gentle rain that fell that day freshened up one of the most beautiful panoramas of natural scenery I ever beheld. It was a sight seldom to be witnessed, never to be forgotten.

That night at Emmittsburg, with its recollections, is to me as sacred as holy writ. The excitement, the knowledge of the great battle soon to be fought; the killing and wounding of many of the brave boys of Ohio and other loyal States of the Union; the wonder what fate awaited us,—were all thoughts that flew through the minds of the soldiers of our army who camped at Emmittsburg on the night of June 30, 1863.

Of my own Sixty-first Regiment I remember that night Colonel Stephen J. McGroarty, Lieutenant Colonel William H. Bown, Major D.C. Beckett and many others who, in the next few days, or afterwards on

Right Flank marker, 61st Ohio, Cemetery Ridge
Photo by Robert G. Carroon

Left and Right Flank markers, 61st Ohio, Cemetery Ridge
(beneath pine trees)
Photo by Robert G. Carroon

the lofty heights of Kennesaw, and at the bloody waters of Peachtree Creek, gave up their lives that this vast Republic might live.

July 1st we marched towards Gettysburg, and the roaring artillery in the distance gave notice that the long-looked-for battle was on. The hurried orders of march, and finally the double quick, brought us into the little village of Gettysburg a little after noon, and a rapid march along the Mummasburg Pike and a deployment into position, with active fighting going on all along the lines, was the situation we experienced.

I cannot refrain from expressing my high admiration for the unrivaled gallantry displayed by our boys upon the first day of this great battle. Ohio was there with the best and bravest of her troops—infantry, cavalry and artillery. Let me particularize for a moment of our immediate command: the Twenty-fifth, Fifty-fifth, Sixty-first, Seventy-third, Seventy-fifth and Eighty-second Ohio—all of these regiments were in the fight on the first day.

The gallantry of our commanders and soldiers has challenged the highest admiration of the Confederate historians. The Ohio soldiers of that day will not forget the illustrious example of our commanders. General Orland Smith, of the Ohio Brigade, yet lives to remember the thrilling incidents of the great first day at Gettysburg. His patriotic devotion to the cause of the Union, his unflinching courage upon the field of battle, his wise and able generalship are remembered by us all.

The gallant General James S. Robinson was a marvel and a tower of strength in commanding his gallant regiment and brigade. His voice, like the roaring lion of the forest, rose above the din of battle in leading his troops into the thickest of the fight.

Colonel Stephen J. McGroarty, of the Sixty-first Ohio, was as brave a man as ever marched to the sound of battle, and his conduct that afternoon is well remembered by those of us that saw him lead his regiment into the battle. All of the commanders of the Twenty-fifth, Fifty-fifth and Seventy-fifth Ohio regiments distinguished themselves and their regiments in the great battle of that afternoon. I want to invite attention to the great battle of the first day. I want my companions who study war history to investigate the great fighting that was done to hold the Confederate army in check that long, hot hellish afternoon of fierce and bloody battle.

The gallant Captain Dilger, with his Ohio Battery, won the admiration of all of us. He was one of the best artillery officers that ever commanded a battery, and lives today at Front Royal, Virginia, and is a prosperous farmer.

Was it not a dispensation of divine Providence that enabled two small corps to hold in check the mighty corps of Ewell and Hill, who outnumbered the Federal Troops at least three to one!

I have often wondered what was the reason that the Confederate army did not follow up the small remnants of the two corps that fell back before overwhelming numbers that afternoon. I have wondered if it might not have been different had Stonewall been there. It is evident that he was the most brilliant and dashing of all the Confederate chieftains. Lee needed such a man at that time. It seems to me Lee lost his best eye when Jackson fell in the great wilderness of Chancellorsville.

But enough of this rambling paper. The writer is proud that victory came to us at Gettysburg; that we have all lived long enough to see the best and greatest of all the nations of the earth in its highest tide of prosperity, and that the Union lives and will live forever, and that its impartial historian will write of the boys who fought for either the blue or the gray; that they will, with the same bravery displayed in the days of the Civil War, fight side by side in the future, as they did in the wars under our beloved McKinley for our newly acquired possessions beyond the sea.

Report on the Battle of Gettysburg

By Lieutenant Colonel William H. H. Bown
61st Ohio Infantry

(First published in Official Records of the War of the Rebellion, Series I, Vol. 27, Pt. 1, Pages 738-739)

Near Warrenton Junction, Va.
August 21, 1863

GENERAL: I have the honor to submit to you, in accordance with orders this day received, a detailed report of the operations of the Sixty-first Regiment Ohio Volunteers, from June 28 to July 25 ultimo, the time of the arrival of the regiment at Warrenton Junction, Va., viz:

June 28.   Remained in camp, near Middletown, Md., until about 4 p.m., when we marched to Frederick City, Md.; weather rainy during the night.

June 29.   Marched from Frederick City to Emmitsburg; weather rainy.

June 30.   Remained in camp at Emmitsburg all day; weather rainy.

July 1.   Still in camp at Emmitsburg. At about 8 a.m. Lieutenant-Colonel Bown was sent to Mechanicstown with 4 commissioned officers and 100 enlisted men. At 9 a.m. the regiment marched from Emmitsburg, and arrived at Gettysburg, Pa., at about 1:30 p.m. The First Corps was already engaging the enemy when we arrived at the town. Having the honor to be the advance regiment of the Third Division, we were ordered on the double-quick through the town and into the open fields. As soon as we arrived on the field, were ordered to deploy as skirmishers. We were no sooner deployed than we engaged the enemy. After a severe skirmish of about half an hour,

Report on the Battle of Gettysburg 55

	we drove them from the open field into the woods. We remained in this position nearly all the afternoon covering a section of Captain Dilger's battery, which he had posted near the line of our skirmishers. Late in the afternoon, the enemy's massed column could be seen emerging from the woods in overwhelming numbers, and being so inferior in numbers compared to the enemy, we were ordered to fall back to the cemetery, upon the south of Gettysburg.
July 2.	Still in position behind the breastworks; very heavy skirmishing in our front. The expedition sent to Mechanicstown returned this morning at 8 o'clock; very heavy cannonading and skirmishing in our front all day.
	At 1 p.m. 3 commissioned officers and 50 enlisted men were sent on picket, and 3 commissioned officers and 50 enlisted men were sent to support Captain Dilger's battery, leaving for duty about 90 enlisted men in the line of the regiment. In the evening, the Sixty-first Ohio and One hundred fifty-seventh New York Volunteers, under command of Colonel McGroarty, were sent to support the Twelfth Corps. Owing to some mistake, we were ordered to our old position behind the breastworks, after having been severely repulsed by the enemy.
July 3.	Still in our old position.
July 4.	Still in our old position with rain.
July 5.	Still in our old position behind the breastworks; marched at 6 p.m., and halted in the woods at 12 midnight.
July 6.	Marched to Emmitsburg, and encamped for the night.
July 7.	Marched from Emmitsburg to Middletown, Md.
July 8.	Marched to Boonsborough, Md.
July 9.	In camp at Boonsborough, Md.
July 10.	Marched to Funkstown, Md.
July 11.	In camp at Funkstown, Md.
July 12.	Marched to Hagerstown, Md.
July 13.	Still at Hagerstown, Md.
July 14.	Marched to Williamsport, Md.
July 15.	Marched to Middletown, Md.
July 16.	Marched to Berlin, Md.
July 17 and 18.	In camp at Berlin, Md.
July 19.	Marched this morning, crossing the Potomac River, to near Leesburg, Va.

July 20.   Marched to near Middleburg, Va.
July 21 and 22.   Still in camp near Middleburg, Va.
July 23.   Marched to near New Baltimore, Va.
July 24.   Still in camp at New Baltimore, Va.
July 25.   Marched to Warrenton Junction, and encamped.

Yours respectfully,

W.H.H. Bown,
Lt. Col. Comdg. Sixty-first Ohio Vol.
Infantry.

Brig. Gen. Hector Tyndale
Commanding First Brigade, Third Division.

Cpl. Augustus Hively, Company C, 61st Ohio Volunteer Infantry
Henry L. Hively Collection, USAMHI

The Boys in Blue at Missionary Ridge

By Leonidas M. Jewett
Formerly Captain 61st Ohio Volunteers
Late Brevet Major U.S.V.

(First published in Sketches of War History 1861–1865 of the Commandery of the State of Ohio, Military Order of the Loyal Legion of the United States, Vol. VI, Pages 89–94)

In the march of American progress since the great struggle for national life took place from Sumter to Appomattox, the American people, many of whom have grown up since then, do not know that this Republic was saved by the valor, patriotism, and courage of the men in whose honor we meet to-day. To honor the officers and soldiers who did their whole duty in this great struggle is the sole and only purpose of this paper.

I can not refrain from expressing my views as to the high character of the officers and men of the Union Army that fought and won the battles of the war for the preservation of the Union from 1861–1865. To this and similar organizations is left the duty of reminding the citizens of this, the greatest government on earth, that they owe their life as a nation to the members of the Union army, dead and living, who saved this Nation from angry waves of secession and treason that dashed against Fort Sumter in 1861. It is a subject that appeals to the loyalty and patriotism of every member of the Loyal Legion, and we must in every possible way emphasize the fact that to the loyal armies of the Union we owe every advantage and blessing we enjoy today.

The men that won these battles are rapidly answering to the last roll call, and those that are left must upon all occasions testify to, and keep before the public, an appreciation of the valor of our soldiers upon the battlefield, and invoke the citizens of a loyal and united country to see in the centuries to come, that our heroes who saved the Nation in the time of its greatest peril and caused the blessings of freedom to spread over every inch of our broad domain, are not forgotten.

There is nothing that ean be said to the grizzled veterans of the war upon the subject I have selected that will be new to them; but there is satisfaction in rehearsing some of the incidents of the great struggle and the principles for which we fought in the Civil War.

You loved the Union then; you love it now. You honored the Union cause by fighting for the preservation of the American Republic of States, that treason in vain tried to break up and destroy. You made a great and glorious record, upon whose every page bristles an account of your unflinching devotion and bravery for the cause of the Union. It was after the experience of might battles and Union victories that some of us from the Army of the Potomac had the honor of joining our comrades of the Cumberland with the Eleventh and Twelfth Corps, under Hooker, Howard, and Slocum and sharing in the honors of Wauhatchie and Brown's Ferry. Soon thereafter there happened an event that was one of the grandest achievements of the Civil War, and as best I can I want to surround you in your memory with the grand army of the Union that fought and won the battle of Missionary Ridge, simply to recall some of the incidents of that eventful day, that is a sacred heritage for the generation that has grown up since the war, and to teach those who will follow them to honor the bravery and patriotism of our Union solders who carried the flag of the Nation to victory.

The grandeur of the eventful day lingers in our memory as one of the most exciting events of the Civil War. The marching of that glorious army of ours from the surroundings of Chattanooga to the foot of Missionary Ridge and up its rocky and mountainous heights was a scene hard to rival upon any battlefield. The steady march of veterans accustomed to the smoke and cloud of battle, with the grand old flag of the Union floating over their heads, the flash of the sunlight upon thousands of gleaming muskets of our soldiers wearing the Union blue are some of the incidents that memory places before us to-night in reviewing the glory and victory of our noble army at Missionary Ridge.

The grandest scene of a lifetime, that impresses a soldier, is to see an army march to the field of battle. It is like the surging waves of the mighty ocean to witness the confident onward march toward the enemy, of old and young, tried, trusty brave American soldiers, which can only be attained by the highest soldierly valor and by actual experience upon the battlefield, and by soldiers who are filled with courage that inspires them to win great and decisive battles. In that column were brave men. They were the pride of the patriotic, union-loving people of the nation, who with their prayers were anxious for the overthrow of treason, and the preservation of the best and greatest of all the nations of the earth. The first battle of the war cleaned out and sent to the rear the officers and men who were unworthy and could not face the dangers of the battlefield. In that magnificent column at Missionary Ridge, marching to death and victory, there were none but brave men, whose courage had been tested at Stone River, Chickamauga, and many other battlefields, and they had the push and spirit that can only be seen in tried and trusted soldiers. Nothing could be grander than the sight on that beautiful November day. The valleys, hills, and mountains of this historic battlefield, beautiful and adorned by one of the grandest panoramas of nature that the human eye ever gazed upon, was an inspiration that seized upon the valor, courage, and patriotism of every soldier who marched in that noble column of blue across the valley to the foot of Missionary Ridge and up its steep and rocky sides to victory. In front of them were steep and difficult heights bristling with almost unassailable fortifications. At the mountain top was the flower and pride of the Confederacy, wide awake and on the alert to destroy, with Confederate shot and shell, our soldiers, who were so soon to engage in acts of valor and bravery never excelled by the soldiers of any country, or clime.

I have referred to a few of these facts to show some of the difficulties that surrounded our boys in winning one of the most brilliant victories of the war. To have stood in that column and marched with it in its grand forward movement to victory was an honor not excelled by any other event of the Civil War. It was a battle, as we all know, in some degree fought and won without orders. The boys did not stop at the foot of the mountain. The defiant enemy at the top of the mountain hurling shot, shell, and musket balls into our advancing ranks raised a spirit of courage in the minds of our noble heroes that caused them to disobey the order to stop at the foot of the mountain, and inch by inch, in the face of almost certain death and destruction, they advanced up the mountain side where the battle was on.

The Blue and the Gray were engaged in one of the fiercest and bloodiest battles of the war; the long roll of musketry and blazing cannon filled every nook and corner of the mountain side, and caused the brave soldiers of the Union to spill their blood in the tangled thicket and forest of the perilous ascent. The torrent of death and destruction rushing down the heights from Confederate musket and cannon was destroying our brave boys, but nothing diminished their bravery and courage. They step upward and onward. They are met by almost insurmountable obstacles in the way of fortifications prepared under the leadership and direction of the engineers of the Confederate service.

But with skill and courage they wind around fallen trees, logs, and fortifications and continue their upward march; the old flag of the Union beautifies the scene of death and destruction; its starry folds are torn with shot, shell, and flying debris; its noble bearers fall in the bloody path; noble soldiers take the places of their fallen comrades, and the old flag proudly floats over our boys as they continue to march up the perilous mountain side. It is a hell-roaring battle of death and destruction, but as the ranks thin the courage and bravery of the boys in blue increase, and amid blazing lines of musketry, shot and shell the steady march of our victorious soldiers is reaching the mountain top. The enemy was amazed. The heroes of many hard-fought battles never witnessed grander fighting or braver soldiers than the boys in blue who were then entering upon the mountain top, and driving from the breastworks and fortifications at the top of the mountain the veteran battalions of Bragg's army. What a glorious day it was for the Union cause, an hour of Union triumph and soldierly devotion to our great and mighty Nation! What a joy it was to think we had such brave and capable soldiers and officers that could win so grand and glorious a victory as that! Think of the obstacles they had to meet, and the dangers they had to encounter! Recalling the charges at Fredericksburg and Gettysburg, it did not seem possible that a front assault could be successfully made upon the heights and fortifications of Missionary Ridge; but the great big fact remains that God Almighty only knows what our noble boys in blue can do in trying and exciting conflicts that demand the highest order of soldierly courage on the part of the participants in great and mighty battles.

I have tried in this paper to emphasize the bravery and courage of the Union soldiers that were in our commands in the great conflict on that eventful November day. I have always felt that no place in the great galaxy of battles that we fought and won for the preservation of the Union could a better position be selected to exhibit the courage and soldierly qualities of our heroes than the grand battle fought on the November day at Missionary Ridge.

I am thankful that some of us yet live to review the incidents of that great and decisive battle of the war, and while I say this, I do not forget grand old fighting Joe Hooker, who, with his noble army in the clouds of the heavens, won the famous battle of Lookout Mountain. In the memories of this eventful day, while we are honoring the Union boys in blue who bore our flag to such a grand victory, we must not forget the grand old commander of the Army of the Cumberland, Major-General George H. Thomas, where the Rock and Sage of Chickamauga became at Missionary Ridge the successful commander of the brave Army of the Cumberland that I have been attempting to describe. What soldier that fought at Missionary Ridge does not venerate the name of Thomas? He was as brave as a lion and as gentle as a child. He was a man that inspired the confidence of his soldiers; they looked upon him as a military father, who had an eye single and alone to the honor and glory of the Union cause. They looked upon him as a commander who would not rashly plunge them into the abyss of death and destruction. He was slow and sure in his methods of command, and in conducting military operations he was never reckless and rash, and at the bottom he was always looking out for the best interests of his soldiers and the Union cause. His genius, ability, and bravery upon the battle commanded unflinching support from his officers and soldiers. The mention of his name commands the highest admiration and respect from every living soldier who fought in that great and glorious column on that November day when the illustrious battle of Missionary Ridge was fought and won.

Lydon of Andersonville

By John McElroy
Late Private, Co. "L"
16th Illinois Volunteer Cavalry

(First published in Andersonville:
A Story of Rebel Military Prisons by John McElroy (Toledo, 1879)

One day in November [1864] orders came in to make out rolls of all those who were born outside the United States and whose terms of service had expired. We held a little council among ourselves as to the meaning of this and concluded that some partial exchange had been agreed on, and the Rebels were going to send back the class of boys whom they thought would be of least value to the Government. Acting on this conclusion the great majority of us enrolled ourselves as foreigners and as having served out our terms. I made out the roll of my hundred and managed to give every man a foreign nativity. Those whose names would bear it were assigned to England, Ireland, Scotland, France, and Germany, and the balance were distributed through Canada and the West Indies. After finishing the roll and sending it out, I did not wonder that the Rebels believed the battles for the Union were fought by foreign mercenaries. The other rolls were made out in the same way, and I do not suppose that they showed five hundred native Americans in the Stockade.

The next day after sending out the rolls, there came an order that all those whose names appeared thereon should fall in. We did so promptly, and as nearly every man in camp was included, we fell in as for other purposes by hundreds and thousands. We were then marched outside and massed around a stump on which stood a Rebel officer, evidently waiting to make a speech. We awaited his remarks with the greatest impatience, but he did not begin until the last division had marched out and came to a parade rest close to the stump. It was the same old story.

"Prisoners, you no longer have any doubt that your Government has cruelly abandoned you; it makes no effort to release you and refuses all our offers of exchange. We are anxious to get our men back and have made every effort to do so, but it refuses to meet us on any reasonable grounds. Your Secretary of War has said that the Government can get along very well without you, and General Halleck has said that you were nothing but a set of blackberry pickers and coffee boilers, anyhow. You're already endured much more than it could expect of you; you served it faithfully during the term you enlisted for, and now, when it is through with you it throws you aside to starve and die. You also can have no doubt that the Southern Confederacy is certain to succeed in securing its independence. It will do this in a few months. It now offers you an opportunity to join its service, and if you serve it faithfully to the end, you will receive the same rewards as the rest of its soldiers. You will be taken out of here, be well clothed and fed, given a good bounty, and at the conclusion of the War receive a land warrant for a nice farm. If you..."

But we had heard enough. The sergeant of our division—a man with a senatorian voice—sprang out and shouted, "Attention, First Division!" We sergeants of hundreds repeated the command down the line. Shouted he, "First Division about..." Said we: "First Hundred about...."; "Second Hundred about...."; "Third Hundred about..."; "Fourth Hundred about...." etc., etc. Said he.... "Face!"

Ten sergeants repeated "Face!" one after the other, and each man in the hundreds turned on his heel. Then our leader commanded—"First Division, forward! March!" and we strode back into the Stockade, followed immediately by all the other divisions, leaving the orator still standing on the stump.

The Rebels were furious at this curt way of replying. We had scarcely reached our quarters when they came in with several companies with loaded guns and fixed bayonets. They drove us out of our tents and huts into one corner under the pretense of hunting axes and spades, but in reality to steal our blankets and whatever else they could find that they wanted, and to break down and injure our huts, many of which, costing us days of patient labor, they destroyed in pure wantonness.

We were burning with the bitterest indignation. A tall, slender man named Lydon*, a member of the 61st Ohio—a rough, uneducated

---

*John McElroy, in his original account written fifteen years after the events recorded, refers to Lydon as Lloyd; however, the patriotic speaker of his account was Corporal William Lydon of Company B, 61st Ohio Volunteer Infantry, who was captured at the Battle of Chancellorsville on May 2, 1863. Described in his enlistment papers as 5' 4½" in height with blue eyes and fair hair he apparently died in Andersonville. His wife, Bridget, applied for a pension on September 26, 1863, having heard a rumor of her husband's death. She had an infant son who was adopted by the man she later married by the name of Fitzgerald. William and Bridget's son, known as J. D. Fitzgerald received a pension in 1879 following his mother's death.

fellow, but brim full of patriotism and manly common sense, jumped up on a stump and poured out his soul in rude but fiery eloquence: "Comrades," he said, "do not let the blowing of these Rebel whelps discourage you; pay no attention to the lies they have told you today; you know well that our Government is too honorable and just to desert any one who serves it; it has not deserted us; their hell-born Confederacy is not going to succeed. I tell you that as sure as there is a God who reigns and judges in Israel, before the spring breezes stir the tops of these blasted old pines their —— Confederacy and all the lousy graybacks who support it will be so deep in hell that nothing but a search warrant from the throne of God Almighty can ever find it again. And the glorious old Stars and Stripes..."

Here we began cheering tremendously. A Rebel captain came running up, and said to the guard, who was leaning on his gun, gazing curiously at Lydon:

"What in hell are you standing gaping for? Why don't you shoot the god-damned Yankee son of a bitch?" and snatching the gun away from him, cocked and leveled it at Lydon, but the boys near by jerked the speaker down from the stump and saved his life.

We became fearfully wrought up. Some of the more excitable shouted out to charge the line of guards, snatch their guns away from them and force our way through the gates. The shouts were taken up by others, and as if in obedience to the suggestion, we instinctively formed in line-of-battle facing the guards. A glance down the line showed me an array of desperate, tensely drawn faces, such as one sees who looks at men when they are summoning up all their resolution for some deed of great peril. The Rebel officers hastily retreated behind the line of guards, whose faces blanched, but they leveled their muskets and prepared to receive us.

Captain Bowes, who was overlooking the prison from an elevation outside, had, however, divined the trouble at the outset and was preparing to meet it. The gunners, who had shotted their pieces and trained them upon us when we came out to listen to the speech, had again covered us with them and were ready to sweep the prison with grape and canister at the instant of command. The long roll was summoning the infantry regiments back into line, and some of the cooler-headed among us pointed these facts out and succeeded in getting the line to dissolve again into groups of muttering, sullen-faced men. When this was done, the guards marched out, by a cautious, indirect maneuver, so as not to turn their backs to us.

It was believed that we had some among us who would like to avail themselves of the offer of the Rebels, and that they would try to inform the Rebels of their desires by going to the gate during the night and speaking to the Officer-of-the-Guard. A squad armed themselves with clubs and laid in wait for these. They succeeded in catching several—snatching some of them back even after they had told the guard their wishes in a tone so loud that all near could hear distinctly. The Officer-of-the-Guard rushed in two or three times in a vain attempt to save the would-be deserter from the cruel hands that clutched him and bore him away to where he had a lesson in loyalty impressed upon the fleshiest part of his person by a long, flexible strip of pine, wielded by very willing hands.

After this was kept up for several nights different ideas began to prevail. It was felt that if a man wanted to join the Rebels, the best way was to let him go and get rid of him. He was of no benefit to the Government and would be of none to the Rebels. After this no restriction was placed upon any one who desired to go outside and take the oath. But very few did so, however, and these were wholly confined to the Raider crowd.

Index

This history of the 61st Ohio concerns the regiment on every page.

A

Alexandria, Virginia, 35
Allatoona Mountain, Georgia, 12
Ames, Adelbert, 8, 9
Andersonville Prison, 46, 63
Antietam, 5
Appomattox, Virginia, 46, 58
Aquia Creek, Virginia, 5, 23, 41, 44
Arbuckle, John, 2
Army of the Cumberland, 1, 27, 29, 59, 61
Army of the Potomac, 1, 49, 50, 59
Atlanta, Georgia, 14, 29, 49
Averysboro, North Carolina, 34

B

Baltimore, Maryland, 50
Bangor, Maine, 24
Banks, Nathaniel P., 5, 19
Banks' Ford, 46, 49
Barlow, Francis C., 25
Beckett, David C., 4, 12, 13, 19, 30, 50
Belle Isle Prison, 46
Bending, Henry R., 9
Bentonville, North Carolina, 1, 14
Berlin, Maryland, 55
Birney, David B., 49
Black River (North Carolina), 34
Blumenthal, Frederick, 5
Bohlen, Henry, 2, 19
Bonaparte, Napoleon, 49
Boonsborough (Boonsboro), Maryland, 55
Bown, William H. H., 11, 17, 19, 27, 31, 50, 54, 55

Brent, Edward V., 9
Brevard, Henry, 10
Bridgeport, Alabama, 10, 27, 28
Broad River, 34
Brooks, William T. H., 46
Brown's Ferry, 59
Bull Run, battle of, 17, 21, 25, 46, 47, 48
Burnside, Ambrose, 5, 23, 28
Burnt Hickory, Georgia, 30
Buschbeck, Adolphus, 25

C

Calhoun, Georgia, 29
Camp Chase, Ohio, 1, 2, 11, 17, 18, 37
Camp Dennison, Ohio, 11, 27, 29
Cape Fear River, 34
Cassville, Georgia, 12, 29, 30
Catlett's Station, Virginia, 47
Catoctin Mountains, Virginia, 49
Cawtaba River, 34
Cedar Mountain, 19
Cemetery Hill (Gettysburg, Pennsylvania), 8, 9
Centerville, Virginia, 5, 21, 47, 48
Chain Bridge, 21
Chancellorsville, battle of, 1, 6, 23, 24, 25, 26, 41, 46, 47, 49, 50
Chancellorsville House, 25, 41, 44
Chantilly, Virginia, 5, 21
Chattahoochie River, 13, 14, 30, 31
Chattanooga, Tennessee, 10, 11, 13, 27, 28, 29, 31, 49, 59
Chesterfield, South Carolina, 34
Chickamauga, 59

Cincinnati, Ohio, 6, 13, 31
Colston, Raleigh E., 45
Columbia, South Carolina, 34
Columbus, Ohio, 1, 10, 14
Corcoran, J. Edward P., 5, 17
Couch, Darius N., 46
Cross Keys, 25
Crouse, David W., 4
Culp's Farm. *See* Kolb's Farm
Culp's Hill (Gettysburg, Pennsylvania), 8
Cumberland Valley, 49

D

Daily, Amos, 10
Dallas, Georgia, 12, 30
Davisboro, Georgia, 32
Decatur, Georgia, 32
Devens, Charles N., 23, 24, 26, 42, 43
Dilger, Herbert, 6, 24, 25, 26, 52
Dilger's Battery, 4, 6, 8, 9, 19, 24, 25, 55
Dole, George, 8
Dowdall's Tavern, Virginia, 25, 41, 46

E

East Chickamauga River, 11
Eatonton, Georgia, 32
Edisto River, 34
Edward's Ferry, 48
Emmitsburg, Maryland, 6, 8, 50, 54, 55
Etowah River, 12, 30
Ewell, Richard S., 52

F

Fairfax Court House, 5
Fairview, Virginia, 25, 26, 46
Falmouth, Virginia, 5, 21
Fayetteville, North Carolina, 34
Fishel, David, 12
Fitzgerald, J. D., 64
Forrest, Nathan B., 27
Fort Sumter, 58
Frederick, Maryland, 49, 54
Fredericksburg, battle of, 1, 5, 6, 23, 49, 61
Freeman's Ford, 1, 2, 4, 19
Fremont, John C., 2, 18
French, William H., 49, 50
Front Royal, Virginia, 52
Funkstown, Maryland, 53

G

Gainesville, Virginia, 19
Garrett, John, 32
Geary, John W., 14, 30, 34
Georgia Troops
 Dole's Brigade, 8

Germania Ford, 41
Gettysburg, Pennsylvania, 1, 6, 7, 8, 9, 10, 26, 49, 52, 53, 54, 55, 61
Gilchrist, Alexander, 18
Goldsboro, North Carolina, 14, 34, 35
Goose Creek, Virginia, 48
Graham, Charles K., 42
Grant, Ulysses S., 28
Great Pede River, 34
Groveton, Virginia, 19
Gum Springs, Virginia, 48

H

Hagerstown, Maryland, 9, 26, 55
Halleck, Henry W., 49, 50
Hamilin, Augustus C., 24
Hamilton, Ohio, 17
Hardie, James A., 50
Harper's Ferry, Virginia, 49
Harris, George H., 16, 18, 30
Hartwood Church, Virginia, 5, 23, 47
Hassler, Warren, 6
Hill, Ambrose P., 45, 52
Hively, Augustus, 57
Hood, John B., 2
Hooker, Joseph, 11, 13, 26, 30, 41, 42, 46, 49, 50, 59
Howard, Oliver O., 6, 9, 11, 23, 24, 26, 27, 42, 43, 44, 45, 46, 59

I

Illinois Troops
 Infantry
  82nd, 6, 8, 9, 11, 12
  101st, 11, 29
Indiana Troops
 Artillery
  5th Indiana Battery, 11, 29

J

Jackson, Thomas J. "Stonewall," 19, 23, 41, 42, 43, 45, 46, 47, 53
Jeffersonville, Maryland, 48
Jewett, Leonidas M., 16, 17, 20, 47, 58
Johnson, Andrew, 35

K

Kearney, Philip, 21
Kelly's Ford, 6, 19, 23
Kennesaw Mountain, Georgia, 12, 13, 30, 52
Kingston, Georgia, 12, 30
Kirtz, George W., 24
Kniepe, Joseph F., 13
Knoxville, Tennessee, 10, 28

Index

Kolb's Farm, Georgia, 12, 30
Krzyzanowski, Waldimir, 8

L

Lancaster, Ohio, 17
Law, Evander M., 2
Lee, Fitzhugh, 45
Lee, John C., 25, 42
Lee, Robert E., 6, 26, 41, 45, 46, 49, 50, 53
Leesburg, Virginia, 48, 55
Leifer, Jacob, 10
Leifer, Marcus, 10
Libby Prison, 46
Lincoln, Abraham, 17, 50
Little Petersburg, Virginia, 18
Longstreet, James, 4
Look Out Creek, 10
Lookout Mountain, Tennessee, 28, 61
Look Out Valley, 27
Lost Mountain, Georgia, 12
Louisville, Kentucky, 35
Luray Court House, Virginia, 19
Lydon, Bridget, 64
Lydon, William, 64

M

Mackey, James, 24
Manassas Junction, Virginia, 47
Marietta, Georgia, 13, 30
McClellan, George B., 4, 48
McGroarty, Stephen J., 1, 2, 4, 5, 10, 13, 17, 18, 19, 25, 27, 30, 31, 35, 36, 37, 50, 52, 55
McGroarty, William, 10, 27
McKinley, William, 53
McLean, Nathaniel C., 23, 26, 42, 44
McMains, Robert S., 26
McMinnville, Tennessee, 27
Meade, George G., 49, 50
Mechanicstown, Maryland, 54, 55
Mell, Joseph R. P., 9
Middleburg, Virginia, 56
Middletown, Maryland, 18, 48, 49, 54, 55
Military Order of the Loyal Legion, 8, 27, 58
Milledgeville, Georgia, 32
Miller, Thaddeus K., 10, 16
Milroy, Robert H., 18
Missionary Ridge, 1, 10, 28, 58, 59, 61, 62
Monocacy Valley, Maryland, 48
Monteith Swamp, Georgia, 32
Moore, William S., 9, 17, 26
Moorefield, Virginia, 18
Mt. Olive Church, Georgia, 30

Mullen, Theodore, 18, 30
Mysenberg, Theodore A., 27

N

New Baltimore, Virginia, 56
New Creek, West Virginia, 18
New Hope Church, Georgia, 30
New York Troops
  Infantry
    45th, 6, 9, 11, 18
    50th, 9
    143rd, 11, 12, 29
    157th, 6, 9, 55
Newcomb, Edward H., 31

O

Oak Hill (Gettysburg, Pennsylvania), 8, 52
Ogeechee River, 32
Ohio Troops
  Infantry
    1st, 29
    2nd, 21
    25th, 8, 52
    50th, 17
    52nd, 17
    55th, 18, 52
    61st, Passim
    73rd, 25
    82nd, 11, 14, 16, 19, 28, 29, 30, 31, 32, 35, 52
Oostenaula River, 29
Orange and Alexandria Rail Road, 10, 27
Otto, August, 9

P

Pace's Ferry, Georgia, 31
Pea Vine Creek, Georgia, 29
Peabody, John H., 6
Peachtree Creek, 1, 4, 13, 31, 35, 52
Pearce, Enoch, 17
Pennsylvania Troops
  Infantry
    74th, 6, 8, 9, 18, 25
Pickett's Charge, 9, 49
Pine Knob, Georgia, 30
Pleasanton, Alfred E., 45
Pope, John, 2, 5, 19, 20
Porter, Fitz John, 5
Potomac River, 4, 8, 55
Purysburg, South Carolina, 34

R

Raleigh, North Carolina, 35
Rallston, Alfred H., 2
Rappahannock River, 2, 5, 6, 19, 23, 41, 47

Reno, Jesse L., 48
Resaca, Georgia, 11, 12, 29
Reynolds, James M., 9, 26
Richardson, William P., 25
Richmond, Virginia, 14, 35
Riley, Robert, 25
Ringgold, Georgia, 28
Robertsville, South Carolina, 14, 34
Robinson, James S., 11, 13, 25, 29, 30, 31, 35, 52
Rocky Face Ridge, Georgia, 11, 29
Rocky Mount, North Carolina, 34
Rodes, Robert E., 8, 45
Romney, Virginia, 18

S

Salem Church, 16
Salomon, Edward S., 8
Saluda River, 34
Sand Mountain, 27
Sandersonville, Georgia, 14, 32
Savannah, Georgia, 14, 32, 34
Schimmelfennig, Alexander, 4, 5, 6, 21
Schleich, Newton, 1, 4, 17
Schultz, Daniel, 16, 18, 24
Schurz, Carl, 4, 5, 8, 9, 21, 23, 26, 42, 43
Sears, Stephen, 6
Second Bull Run, battle of, 1, 4, 5, 19, 20
Sedgewick, John, 46, 49
Sherman, William T., 14, 28, 32
Sickles, Daniel E., 42, 45, 46, 49
Sigel, Franz, 4, 5, 21, 26
Sister's Ferry, Georgia, 14
Slocum, Henry W., 42, 49, 59
Smith (Schmidt), Jacob, 5
Smith, Orland, 25, 52
Smith, William A., 12
Snake Creek Gap, Georgia, 11, 29
South Mountain, Maryland, 48
Spellman, Cornelius, 24
Sperryville, Virginia, 2, 19, 21
Spitzer (Sutler), 18
Springfield, Georgia, 32
Stafford Court House, Virginia, 5, 6, 23, 26, 47
Stafford Heights, 47, 49
Stanley, David S., 11
Stanton, Edwin M., 50
Stilesboro, Georgia, 30
Stone River, 59
Strasburg, Virginia, 2, 18
Stuart, James E. B., 46
Sullivan, Daniel O., 9
Sulphur Springs, Virginia, 4, 19

T

Tennessee Troops (U.S.)
  Infantry
    4th, 27
Thomas, George H., 27, 61
Thompson, David, 31
Trenton, Georgia, 27
Trickum Post Office, Georgia, 11, 29
Trimble, Isaac R., 2
Tyndale, Hector, 28, 55

U

United States Army Corps
  I, 2, 8, 54
  III, 49
  IV, 11, 12, 29
  XI, 1, 6, 8, 9, 10, 23, 24, 27, 29, 42, 44, 45, 46, 59
  XII, 10, 27, 29, 49, 55, 59
  XIV, 35
  XX, 11, 14, 29, 31, 34, 35
United States' Ford, 44

V

Van Alen, James H., 42
Virginia Troops (U.S.)
  Infantry
    8th, 18
Von Amsberg, George, 6, 8
Von Steinwehr, Adolph W. A. F., 42, 43

W

Wallace, Frederick S., 2, 5, 6, 9, 15, 16
Walthall, Edward C., 13
Warrenton Junction, Virginia, 54, 55
Warrenton, Virginia, 4, 5
Washington, D.C., 5, 14, 21, 35
Wateree, River, 34
Waterloo Bridge, Virginia, 4, 19
Wauhatchie Valley, Tennessee, 10, 27, 28
Weaversville, Virginia, 9
Wheeler, Joseph, 27
White Sulphur Springs, Virginia, 19
Williams, Alpheus S., 11, 13, 30, 31
Williams, Daniel W., 9, 26
Williamsport, Maryland, 53
Winnsboro, South Carolina, 34
Wygram, George W., 17

Y

Yeazel, James, 44